honoring our animals

365 MEDITATIONS FOR HEALING AFTER PET LOSS

Beth Bigler

wellfleet
press

Contents

Introduction || 5

How to Use This Book || 6

New Beginnings
January || 10

February || 28

Awakenings
March || 46

April || 64

May || 80

Abundance
June || 98

July || 116

August || 132

Release

September || 150

October || 168

November || 184

Celebration and Reflection

December || 202

Grieving Guardian Glossary || 220

Grief Feelings Wheel || 221

Index || 222

Acknowledgements || 226

About the Author || 227

Introduction

Dear Grieving Guardian,

Your beloved's transition may feel like the worst thing that's ever happened to you. It may even feel more harrowing than human grief. While the gap left in your heart can't be filled, in time, you can learn to weave your grief into the tapestry of your life. But how?

When my cat Arnie died, I was completely shattered. It was harder than any death I had ever experienced and completely destabilizing. A love so deep and true couldn't just evaporate because Arnie wasn't in his physical form. So, I decided to keep our connection growing and cultivated ways to feel connected to my beloved companion. My determination to survive also led me to search for pet loss grief counseling and deep, inner exploring. I learned how to allow my grief to move with me, to discover resonant grief expressions, and to gradually integrate Arnie's earthside absence into my life. And today, many years after his transition, I can say I feel even closer to him than I ever have—our love story has no end.

The transformative help I received also propelled me (alongside Arnie) to carry this mission to other grieving animal guardians, which steered me to begin my private pet loss grief counseling practice: Honoring Our Animals.

Taking small daily steps to connect with our feelings, our beloveds, and ourselves allows us to feel empowered and confident, even in the most overwhelming moments. I bring my own training, experience, passion, and stories of thousands of grievers to offer you my most comforting insights and empowerment in these pages.

Welcoming these meditations into your life is a powerful and courageous act of honoring your beloved and yourself as you continue to grieve. May these words feel like true friends who walk beside you, encouraging your next best step as you integrate your beloved's transition into your life.

Thank you for taking care of yourself and your beloved by supporting your grief. You are not alone.

And thank you, beloved companions, for all you revealed to us during your earthly lives and all you continue to give as we evolve and expand. Thank you for loving us so fiercely. We are truly honored to be yours forever.

How to Use This Book

The meditations in this book are designed to help you cultivate coping skills, inspire self-discovery, and encourage your continuing connection with your beloved.

You will notice I use specific terms throughout the book to talk about grief, such as "beloved" instead of "pet," "transition" instead of "death," and "guardian" instead of "pet owner." You may also notice that I often refer to our current relationship with our beloveds in the present tense. This is because I see our bond as ongoing instead of in the past. Sometimes, I use the past tense—for me, it's a personal choice about when it feels right to use it. There is no right or wrong, and, as with all language around grief, experiment and choose what feels most supportive to you. Refer to the grieving guardian glossary, which highlights terms I prefer to use throughout the book, at any time (page 220).

At the end of each meditation is an invitation for a next step, such as a journaling prompt, activity, affirmation, or reflection. I can't overstate the benefit of a notebook or drawing pad to jot notes, doodle, include photographs that remind you of your beloved, and respond to invitations. The invitations are designed to be a practical tool to integrate your grief into your life. Attempt them only if it feels affirming to do so. You're not "doing it wrong" if you don't feel up to completing an invitation.

Seasonal transitions can be difficult, with their memories, expectations, and the pain of time passing—realizing it's one more new season your beloved won't be with you—which is why each quarter of the year has its own introduction.

You'll also find a grief feelings wheel (page 221) that you can use to identify where you are throughout your experience and to respond to meditations that utilize it as a tool.

Just as there is no right or wrong way to grieve, there is no right or wrong way to use this book.

You may want to experience one reflection per day or read through it in one sitting. Or you may prefer to use the index on page 222 to target the emotions or curiosities you are experiencing in any given moment. Do what feels authentic to you.

This is a place for validation, understanding, and hope, and your permission slip to express your grief and mourn your beloved.

As these months unfold, observe how your body, mind, and spirit may desire more inward focus. The start of the New Year often brings expectations for action and productivity, but why not welcome it with a readiness for interiority and quiet instead? Allow this new time to steer you into moments of inner reflection.

Encourage a soothing environment and stability around yourself, allowing for renewal and introspection. Instead of setting ambitious goals, embrace consistency and curl into a more denlike peace. Hold yourself still in the winds of daily life.

Let yourself feel your emotions and take the time to reflect on what your needs and wants are during this time of newness. Once you are clear on what you need, you can open yourself up to the possibility of new beginnings and what new things may unfold for you during your time of healing.

As your beloved's love and support of you was as consistent as the tide, during these months, pinpoint current areas of your life where greater consistency could offer more nurturing and constancy, and take small action steps to create more of this steadiness in your life. All you need is one step, one promise to create more steadiness in your life.

Honor your sorrow and emerging healing. Acknowledge the bittersweetness of your experience. Speak your beloved's name with gratitude and thank the universe for the wisdom you gained through your relationship.

January 1

Your beloved's story is more than their last day. In grief, you may find yourself returning to the events and images of the last time you saw them. Bringing balance to your brain and heart by remembering, sharing, and celebrating the tapestry of stories that illustrate your beloved's life is a loving act of tenderness. Their earthside days were filled with joy, excitement, and gratitude. Amplify those moments and allow them to be a comforting quilt as you grieve.

♥ **INVITATION:** Write a letter to your beloved that tells them the story of their life with you.

January 2

Your daily routine with your beloved is a cherished part of your life, and maintaining familiar rituals can comfort your mind, especially in early grief. Continue including your beloved in your day-to-day, honoring them as an important ancestor within your family. This practice fosters a sense of continuity and connection as you adjust to their physical absence.

♥ **INVITATION:** Keep "greeting" your beloved when you come home and saying "farewell" when you leave, using familiar phrases. Place a favorite photo by the door and give it a love tap each time you come and go.

January 3

You are the only one who knows your beloved on a soul level. Trust your instinct, heart, and intuition to connect with their voice and guidance. Your spirit understands them with the same clarity it always has. Even if grief makes it difficult to hear them, remain open to listening and exploring together. Believe that you can continue to give and receive from them at any moment.

♥ **INVITATION:** Write a letter to yourself from your beloved, in their voice, and ask them to share anything they'd like to tell you.

January 4

It's hard to wake up in a world without your beloved. You might find yourself asking, *Can I even survive this?* If you do nothing else within your grief, you must survive. You don't have to be productive, nice, accommodating, or strong. You just have to survive it. One breath, one second, one minute, one hour at a time. You will make it through. You will find a way. It takes guts, determination, and persistence to survive the loss of a beloved. You've got this.

♥ **INVITATION:** What do you imagine would be your beloved's best advice about survival?

January 5

What are your beloved's core values? Adventure, assertiveness, curiosity, fun, or non-conformity might be some. What do you discover in these? Take stock of yours: What excites you? What brings you peace? What matters to you? Whether your values are empathy, service, courage, growth, collaboration, integrity, creativity, or others, reconnecting with these values is crucial to finding your purpose.

♥ **INVITATION:** Write an intention for yourself, your beloved, and your relationship together based on your identified core values. Use this statement to recharge and reinvigorate yourself when you're feeling lost.

January 6

When a beloved transitions, it's not just their physical form you mourn. Like ripples in a pond, secondary losses extend outward—loss of dreams, plans, and milestones you imagined in their presence. Your sense of purpose, identity, and meaning might feel unsteady, as if the currents have altered. Even your confidence, safety, and faith can waver, making the world feel different.

♥ **INVITATION:** List the secondary losses you've experienced and create a ritual, meditation, or journaling practice to honor each one.

January 7

Keep using your beloved's name and find gentle ways to have it spoken and honored by others. Their name is one of the most beautiful sounds to your ears, like vibrant wonder, and keeping it alive celebrates your connection.

♥ **INVITATION:** Use their name at the coffee shop, write it in the sand or snow, find songs with it in the lyrics, engrave it on jewelry, use it for reservations, name a future family member in their honor, or simply repeat it aloud to yourself whenever you need a boost.

January 8

Your surviving animals grieve too, and it can feel like watching them navigate a maze, searching for a path that no longer exists. As they show changes in mood, appetite, or behavior, we might feel powerless. But you can be their guide, offering gentle comfort, maintaining routines, and offering extra affection to help them feel more secure in their grief.

♥ **INVITATION:** Start daily conversations with your surviving animals, sharing memories, reassuring them they're safe, and reminding them that you're there to support them through their sorrow.

January 9

Speaking out loud is a powerful support tool. When you speak, your brain engages more deeply, reinforcing the messages you send. Whether you're talking to your beloved, offering kind affirmations to yourself, or sharing a story that makes you smile, let your voice be a source of comfort and grounding in your sorrow.

♥ **INVITATION:** When the weight of grief feels unbearable, repeat this affirmation out loud: *I carry my beloved with me and our connection brings me strength.*

January 10

You may have noticed signs from your beloved, such as a familiar scent on the breeze, a dream where they visit you, or feeling their presence in a quiet moment. If you haven't experienced this yet, don't worry. Signs often take time to manifest, sometimes appearing months or even years later. Stay open to the possibility, and you may be surprised by how your beloved communicates their love. These signs, like whispers from nature, affirm that your bond transcends physical boundaries, offering comfort and healing.

♥ **INVITATION:** Keep a list of signs, coincidences, and visitations from your beloved. Revisit this list when you are feeling disconnected and ask openly for more of the signs already received. Many times, signs repeat themselves!

January 11

Grief is unpredictable and filled with unexpected feelings. You may be thinking: *Is it normal to miss them so much? Am I weird to dread putting their food bowl away?* All the feelings you are experiencing as you integrate this loss into your life are common and natural. Be patient with yourself as you grieve the transition of your beloved. Your feelings are valid, common, and a testimony to the beautiful bond you share.

♥ **INVITATION:** The next time you notice these types of judgments arising, ask yourself out loud: *How is this serving me?* then turn your focus to a more loving opinion about your grief, such as, *I honor my grief with compassion and patience.*

January 12

A silent house can be one of the loudest reminders of your grief. The absence of day-to-day patter, chatter, and play can feel crushing. To ease the hush, welcome soothing sounds into your space. Music, ocean waves, binaural beats, rain, or crackling fire can offer a gentle presence, filling the silence with something comforting and familiar.

♥ **INVITATION:** Consider setting a timer or turning on these sounds before you arrive home so they're already playing when you walk through the door, easing your transition into the quiet.

January 13

Identify your beloved's signature color and show it! It can also be fun to learn more about the meaning of your chosen hue in terms of color theory, culture, and symbolism. It feels amazing to "choose" your beloved each time you have an option for a color choice. Allow color to paint your grief with celebration and closeness.

♥ **INVITATION:** Incorporate this color into your fashion, accessories, office supplies, kitchen accessories, art projects, or flowers on their altar.

January 14

When overwhelmed, consider the soothing release of the "ahhh" sound. This simple act can stimulate the vagus nerve, release tension in your neck and jaw, and create calming vibrations in your throat and chest. Continuous "ahhhs" for a few minutes can increase oxygen intake and promote relaxation. If it feels awkward at first, be patient—you may be surprised at how good it feels after trying it.

♥ **INVITATION:** Start small with one "ahhh" during your day and work your way up to multiple minutes of "ahhhs."

January 15

Grief can feel like being caught between endless reflections of the past and future. But right here, right now, you can step out of that infinity mirror. Right here, right now, your beloved is safe in your heart. Right here, right now, you are connected in love.

♥ **INVITATION:** When grief pulls you into past or future reflections, place both hands over your heart and repeat, *Right here, right now*... and see what comes. How will you use it today?

January 16

As you wind down for the evening, invite your beloved into your dreams. While an invitation doesn't guarantee their appearance, consistently setting the stage can evoke a powerful connection in your dreamscape. Begin with a short meditation, then gently say: *I invite my beloved into my dreams tonight.* Visualize what you'd like to experience, and remember, your beloved may appear in symbolic forms—through an image, sound, feeling, or words.

♥ **INVITATION:** Write your invitation on a piece of paper, placing it alongside a cherished item of theirs to create a sacred space for a visitation.

January 17

Inviting new experiences into your life can be incredibly powerful for your grief. Whether it's visiting a new place, learning a skill, or changing your route home, small shifts break up routine and activate different parts of your mind. Your brain thrives on novelty, and these fresh experiences can provide a welcome break from the daily grind. Consider planning a day trip or vacation to recharge and reset. Embrace newness whenever possible.

♥ **INVITATION:** List three new things you could plan or do this week.

January 18

You may wonder if your beloved is "okay" after their transition. While this question may not have a clear answer, you can support yourself by imagining where their spirit or essence might be. Picture them playing, sunbathing, or feeling whole and restored. Visualizing what might be happening for them can bring comfort.

♥ **INVITATION:** Ask your beloved how they are doing. You might receive their response in images, words, smells, or a deep feeling of knowing that only exists between you two. Be patient; the answer may take time to reveal itself.

January 19

When grief feels unbearable, take a moment to breathe and feel your beloved's presence. Imagine their comforting touch and loyal gaze, and know they are still by your side, in every moment and heartbeat. They see your struggles and your courage. They are with you, cheering you on, offering comfort in moments of sorrow. Their spirit will always be intertwined with yours, giving you strength even when you feel most vulnerable.

♥ **INVITATION:** Close your eyes and conjure a favorite moment between you and your beloved. Allow yourself to be in the scene and enjoy an adoring moment with them.

January 20

You have limits, like a creek that can only hold so much water before it overflows. Your capacity is finite, and grief takes up a significant part of it—filling your body, mind, heart, and soul. You can't do it all and grieve at the same time. Stop telling yourself you "should" carry on like "normal." Give yourself permission to slow down, reduce commitments, and let the exhaustion and sorrow flow through you. Don't stuff it down. Your bandwidth is precious—use it wisely.

♥ **INVITATION:** What's one thing you can say "no" to that will free up some bandwidth for yourself?

January 21

Laughter releases endorphins and lowers stress hormones, making it a powerful ally during grief. Giving your brain a break from sorrow by inviting in laughter is a true gift to your healing process. Even if it feels awkward at first, make it a point to support more laughter in your life. Whether through a favorite movie, a lighthearted TV show, a comedy skit, or a video of your beloved, seek out what brings you joy and allow moments of lightness amidst your grief.

♥ **INVITATION:** Give yourself the gift of laughter for five minutes today.

January 22

Painting rocks with your beloved's name, favorite toys, or symbols that remind you of them can feel like leaving a trail of love wherever you go. Whether you create a memorial garden or place these rocks in spots your beloved adores, it's like leaving little love notes in the world for others to find or for you to revisit. Consider showcasing their name, the coordinates where you met, favorite phrases, symbols, or your wishes for them now.

♥ **INVITATION:** Document your rock offerings with photos and create a book of all the places you've honored your beloved.

January 23

If you're caught in a cycle of self-criticism, judgment, blame, or overthinking, it might surprise you to learn that this mental squall can be a way to avoid the deep emotions in your body. Sometimes, we retreat into our minds to escape the pain, sorrow, and longing we feel.

♥ **INVITATION:** Today, try tuning in to your body instead. Focus on your feelings, not your thoughts. See what happens when you approach your present emotions with kindness and love, rather than letting your mind take over.

January 24

Sometimes, the silence from those we expect to support us can be deafening. Yet, in that quiet, others often surprise us—reaching out, checking in, sending flowers, or writing a loving note. These are the people to cultivate in your life right now. Grief, like a key, can open doors to new relationships, revealing connections you may not have considered before. Embrace these unexpected companions as you navigate through your journey.

♥ **INVITATION:** Has someone surprised you with their support? Consider inviting them for coffee or tea—either in person or virtually—to nurture that relationship.

January 25

If you're wrestling with a tough "when" subject like "When will I remove my beloved's fur from the couch?" or "When will I donate my beloved's things?" try making a date with yourself three months or six months in the future to discuss it with yourself then. Releasing the pressure valve on making decisions that feel overwhelming can be kind during grief.

♥ **INVITATION:** What topic needs a scheduled check-in with yourself to discuss in the future? Mark a date on your calendar for when you will have a dialogue with yourself about it.

January 26

You are not weak for feeling your emotions. Grieving your beloved might feel like standing in a cyclone—intense, unpredictable, and vigorous. It's easy to mistake this for weakness, but remember: your emotions are like powerful winds, and you have every right to experience them. Grief offers you the opportunity to harness these winds, choosing which to let guide you and which to let pass.

♥ **INVITATION:** Draw a kite and illustrate some of the feelings, emotions, or memories you'd like to release the next time they blow by.

January 27

You will never forget your beloved. They are a part of you forever, woven into your life and deeply embedded in your heart. Their love and presence have shaped you in ways that will always remain, creating a bond that endures beyond their physical presence.

♥ **INVITATION:** Place a glass jar and index cards in your kitchen. Each feeding time, write something on the index card you want to remember about your beloved. Read the cards aloud on their birthday, gotcha day (adoption day), or transition day.

January 28

Grief can make it difficult to articulate what you want. The only thing you might wish for is your beloved to return. In sadness, it's easy to lose touch with your desires. When you feel stricken, a powerful check-in is to ask yourself, *What do I want?* While your wish may not always be possible, tuning in to your wants can be a powerful first step in honoring your needs.

❤ **INVITATION:** State what you want—whether far-fetched, silly, lavish, childish, or simple. Don't judge your desires. There is no right or wrong.

January 29

Identify what you want, then ask yourself, *How do I feel?* This may not be easy. It may require closing your eyes, sitting with your body for a moment, and absorbing the many sensations flowing through you. Often, in sadness, we are asked, "How are you?" but not "How do you feel?" Embrace the power of identifying and naming your feelings.

❤ **INVITATION:** Finish this sentence in your journal or on a piece of paper: I feel ____. You can refer to the grief feelings wheel (see page 221) to help you pinpoint what emotion you're experiencing.

January 30

After naming your feelings, a supportive step is to welcome and validate them. Offering our emotions support for their existence is kind to our most vulnerable self. Acknowledging that feelings are moving through you, rather than being part of your identity, may bring you relief in a moment of chaos or despair.

♥ **INVITATION:** With your feeling identified, reassure yourself and fill out the blank space either in your journal or quietly to yourself. It's okay that I feel _____. I am not a _____ person. My _____ is moving through me. I am allowed to feel _____.

January 31

If you are at a point where you've identified what you want and how you're feeling, and you've validated your right to feel that way, you can go deeper and explore what you need in this moment. It might be something nurturing, soothing, or nourishing. Just as your beloved always knew what you needed, you can begin to meet your own needs in their honor, practicing by addressing them one at a time.

♥ **INVITATION:** Combine this meditation with the January 28 through January 30 meditations and culminate with the question, *What do I need?* Answer each question in the meditations for a powerful daily writing practice you can utilize whenever you feel overwhelmed or want to explore your inner landscape.

27 JANUARY

February 1

One of the things you may miss most is the sound of your beloved. Like a favorite melody, their barks, purrs, chirps, or pattering paws brought comfort and connection. Their absence can feel like a deep chasm in your daily routine. If you have audio files or videos of these cherished sounds, consider gathering them into a special folder—a treasure chest of memories. This way, you can listen to your beloved whenever you need to feel their familiar presence.

❤ **INVITATION:** Set your phone's text alert to one of your beloved's sounds, letting their music fill your day.

February 2

Sometimes, grief opens a door to new dimensions of our own faith, spirituality, and our relationship to the universe. Explorations about the soul, afterlife, Rainbow Bridge, or diverse spiritual traditions may feel supportive. Giving yourself permission to have a complex belief system that doesn't have a fixed set of rules may unlock new spiritual growth and an evolving connection to the universe.

❤ **INVITATION:** What's a spiritual practice or tradition you'd like to learn more about? Write out the answer in your journal.

February 3

Within your swirling emotions, you might feel like it's impossible to have any control. Remind yourself about the key things you can control, such as how you respond to your feelings, how you speak to yourself, and how you can continue to connect with your beloved. Taking agency in these three areas reminds you that even in sorrow, you have the capacity to shape your experience and find meaning on this path.

♥ **INVITATION:** Create a list of all the things that are within your power to control today and choose three to embrace.

February 4

If you're traveling after your beloved's transition, consider bringing a small picture, stuffed animal, or a cherished heirloom that reminds you of them. Having a tangible piece of your beloved with you can offer comfort and connection, even when you're far from home. This simple gesture can make you feel like they're sharing in your new experiences.

♥ **INVITATION:** Take photos of this sacred object on your travels to create a travelogue of new adventures that you and your beloved have experienced together.

February 5

Find a place to sit comfortably. Close your eyes and bring your awareness to your breath. As you inhale, feel yourself inviting in kindness, tenderness, and love, awakening the parts of you that need the most tending. As you exhale, release tension and sorrow. Whisper these words to yourself: *I love myself with each breath I take. My beloved loves me with each breath I take.*

♥ **INVITATION:** Write these on a notecard and place it in one of your beloved's favorite places so you can remember this each time you see the spot.

February 6

Unanswered questions can be frustrating and all-consuming. When you encounter a nagging question that you know can't be answered, place a hand over your heart and gently remind yourself: *That answer is not for me to know at this time.* Allow the universe to hold the possibility of you knowing more at a later moment.

♥ **INVITATION:** Make a list of all your unanswered questions. Seek answers where you can (e.g., from a veterinary professional). For the rest, release them to the universe by burning the piece of paper, burying it, or freeing it into a body of water.

February 7

You can keep sending messages to your beloved, even after they've transitioned. How you do it is entirely up to you. Talking to them keeps your heart and mind connected, like a bridge between worlds. Believe you can hear each other as you ask for advice, share updates, or simply express your love. You can even write letters back and forth with them. Your connection will continue, perhaps even in new, meaningful, and surprising ways.

♥ **INVITATION:** Create a social media account, email address, or dedicated journal just for these communications.

February 8

Browsing profiles of adoptable animals does not betray your beloved or invalidate your grief. It's okay to look for animals that resemble your beloved, have a similar story, or who might be a fit for your family. You aren't causing harm by hope-scrolling cute photos and fantasizing about loving another someday—even if you're not ready for it to actually happen.

♥ **INVITATION:** Release your guilt or fear around this pastime. Continue for as long as it brings your heart joy.

February 9

You may feel like "moving on" is an impossibility or even repugnant. What if you embraced the idea that grief isn't something you "move on" from but something you "move with?" Our grief will accompany us for life, just like our love. The sooner we decide to sway with our grief as it moves with us like the branches of an old, wise tree, the sooner we can release the pressure to be "past" or "through" it.

♥ **INVITATION:** Take one small action step that honors the "move with" mindset.

February 10

If you have a special event, such as a wedding or birthday party coming up and you want to incorporate your beloved into it, here are a few reminders for how to uplift their presence: include photos of them as table decorations, make a toast to them with a signature cocktail or mocktail named for them, incorporate them into your favors, collect money for your favorite animal charity in their name, or wear a piece of jewelry with their name on it.

♥ **INVITATION:** What events are upcoming this year where you can incorporate your beloved?

February 11

Whenever anyone asks, "How can I help?" or says "If you need anything, I'm here," be ready with a specific ask. People who love you likely want to support you but may not know how. Give your inner circle an opportunity to show up for you in this tender time.

♥ **INVITATION:** Try this ask if you're not sure where to start: *Can I share a story about my beloved next time we're together? I love talking about their life.*

February 12

A powerful legacy is creating acts of kindness in your beloved's name. How can you enhance the joy and love your beloved brought to your life through giving to others? You may do something kind for your veterinary or animal care professionals, a rescue, or even a stranger. Enjoy the closeness you feel with your beloved as you cultivate joy in others.

♥ **INVITATION:** Volunteer for an organization you believe in or leave an encouraging Post-it Note in public for someone to find—signed from your beloved!

February 13

Write a love letter to your beloved. You might recall a favorite day you spent together or the quirks about them that always made you laugh. You might thank them for any signs received and for the life lessons they taught you. Whatever you choose to express, know that your words are helping continue the conversation with your beloved and are an adoring tribute to how dear you are to each other.

♥ **INVITATION:** Write a love letter in response to yourself in your beloved's voice.

February 14

Repeat this affirmation to yourself to connect with your beloved:
I cherish the warmth you brought into my life. I am forever connected to you. You may not be earthside, but your presence is felt. Your love is my fortress, a shelter that transition can never take away. Today I will create new memories, inspired by the love you have shown me. Your legacy is one of kindness and compassion, guiding me to spread warmth in the world.

♥ **INVITATION:** What would you like to add to this affirmation to personalize it for your beloved?

February 15

If your grief includes not knowing where your beloved is—whether after a natural disaster or because they slipped from your care—remember that their absence doesn't diminish their love for you or the wonderful life you shared. It isn't personal. Your lifetime of love and care remains intact, even without their physical presence. Like a beacon, continue to send love to them and yourself, releasing blame. You didn't mean for this to happen.

♥ **INVITATION:** Consider a ritual where you send love and vibrant energy to your beloved, affirming your bond.

February 16

Grieving can feel like being caught in a never-ending echo, where every emotion reverberates and amplifies. You might strain to hear something familiar, trying to make sense of the noise or grasping for direction. It's like standing in a vast cavern, yet even in this clanging echo, you can feel your beloved's presence like a clear, steady voice, guiding you. Heart to heart, they remain your true north, helping you find your way, as they always have—and always will.

♥ **INVITATION:** Find a place with a great echo and shout your beloved's name into the void!

February 17

Did you ever admire your beloved's ability to meander effortlessly through the world? Today, experiment with taking a destination-free stroll with your beloved. Set an intention to connect with them before the walk. Bring a talisman that reminds you of them to carry, such as a collar or favorite toy. Invite the breeze to graze your cheek, explore smells, or touch interesting textures you encounter. Allow play and spontaneity as you wander.

♥ **INVITATION:** Ask your beloved questions about what to explore next, such as, *Would it feel good if we go right at the waterfall or continue along the mountain path?*

February 18

Anger wants to be discharged from your body. When a larger physical release isn't possible, consider channeling your anger onto the page through writing. It's powerful and healing to give your anger a voice, even if it's uncomfortable. Start a list where every sentence begins with *I am angry because . . .* and keep filling in the blanks until you've released all the anger you're holding in that moment.

♥ **INVITATION:** Take this list to a secluded place and read or scream it out loud, then tear it up to further release your anger.

February 19

As time passes, scrolling through your phone to find photos of your beloved may feel like reaching deeper into a memory well. If it feels right, consider copying your favorite photos to your camera roll so they're always at the top, ready to bring comfort when you need it. You might also create a special folder filled with cherished images, videos, and sound recordings—a smile file you can open anytime you need a reminder of the love that still shines brightly.

♥ **INVITATION:** What step can you take to make your phone a more comforting space for your grief?

February 20

Creating a consistent sleep routine is crucial. Keep your bedroom cool and stop all screen time at least two hours before bed to calm your mind. Develop a soothing ritual—whether it's a warm bath, skincare routine, gentle stretching, word searches, adult coloring books, or reading—to help you unwind.

♥ **INVITATION:** Before bed, take a moment to connect intentionally with your beloved by writing, speaking, or holding one of their cherished items. This mindful approach creates a peaceful environment, allowing your body and heart the rest they need to rejuvenate.

February 21

Grief expressions are as varied as the waves in an ocean, each with its own rhythm and force. Be gentle with yourself and avoid judging what brings you comfort. Whether it's screaming in your car, planning a memorial, singing karaoke, hiking, praying, painting, or sitting in quiet reflection—each act is valid. There's no right or wrong way to navigate these deep waters. What works for you may surprise you, so keep experimenting.

♥ **INVITATION:** What's a grief expression that feels a little "out of the box" for you? Try it today and see how it resonates.

February 22

Sometimes, the kindest act of self-compassion is releasing the expectation that life will return to its old "normal." Like a dragonfly that begins as a water nymph and molts several times before emerging with wings, grief transforms us profoundly. Embracing this change allows you to honor yourself. You are becoming something new while still carrying the essence of who you were.

♥ **INVITATION:** What aspects of your "old" self would you like to bring into your future self? Make a list and consider how to integrate them into who you are now.

February 23

Close your eyes, take a few deep breaths, and focus on your heart. Imagine your beloved's presence, picture a favorite memory, or simply feel their energy around you. Begin with a thirty-second connection and gradually add more time if it feels supportive. This practice can provide comfort and maintain your bond, reminding you that your connection transcends physical boundaries.

♥ **INVITATION:** Set aside five minutes daily to practice this connection, gradually deepening your experience.

February 24

It may be time to set some limits and start sticking up for yourself, like a fortress guarding its inner sanctuary. Let your grief be the catalyst for building boundaries that protect your well-being. There's no better time than now to step up and claim what you truly deserve.

♥ **INVITATION:** Set limits that will best support your healing. Ask yourself: *What do I deserve in my grief? What boundaries will help me stand strong, knowing I am worthy and valuable in this life?*

February 25

Have you ever been told not to feel so sad about your beloved's transition because there are worse tragedies in the world? Or that you "should" be grateful because your beloved lived a long life? These statements, though well-meaning, can feel dismissive. Your grief is real, and it resonates deeply. Comparing your pain to other losses doesn't diminish its significance. Your emotions deserve to be felt fully.

♥ **INVITATION:** List *I am allowed to grieve alongside* . . . and name the internal and external tensions you feel.

February 26

Anytime you hear a "should" come up, like I "should" be handling this better, or I "should" put my beloved's things away, remember this "shoulding" is often judgmental, unsupportive, and untrue. Taming your "shoulds" is a gradual process, and it's okay if it's new to you. No one masters this practice at the start of grief—it's like navigating a dense forest, where untangling complex feelings takes time. Your opportunity to begin is today.

♥ **INVITATION:** Each time you catch yourself saying one of these phrases: "I should," "I have to," "I ought to," or "I need to," replace it with "I aspire to," "It would be kind if I," "I desire to," or "It would be easier if" and notice how much more supportive it feels.

February 27

Your beloved is your greatest teacher. They've shown you love, like a steady heartbeat, offering affection without expecting anything in return. Through them, you've learned acceptance, welcoming every part of yourself without judgment. Most importantly, they've shown you that you are worthy of love, just as you are.

💜 **INVITATION:** Write a list of your beloved's greatest teachings as a reminder of all they have taught you and all they will continue to reveal.

February 28

When someone asks, "How are you doing?" and you're not fine, it can feel like trying to carry a heavy load up a steep hill. Instead of being weighed down by the enormity of the question, try focusing on the present moment. Summing up your entire experience can be impossible but narrowing it down to today—or even just this hour—allows you to be authentic without the burden of the whole journey.

💜 **INVITATION:** Don't wait for someone to ask. Check in with yourself and practice answering, *How am I doing right now?*

February 29

Every four years, you're gifted with a bonus day to connect with your beloved. However you choose to celebrate, this is an extra day for extra love. Say this affirmation to yourself quietly or aloud: *I will leap into love with gratitude for this extra day to celebrate my beloved.*

♥ **INVITATION:** Identify four things you'd like to try in the next four years that you've been too afraid to "leap" into and write a letter to your beloved about starting them. Include that in a relationship time capsule about you and your beloved that you can open on the next leap day.

43

FEBRUARY

There will be moments in your grief that will signal an awakening or a spark of hope, highlighting a contrast to your own inner gloom.

In moments of sadness and deep sorrow, think of a butterfly and remember her journey: starting as a caterpillar, she molts multiple times to grow, forming a chrysalis from within. Inside this protective space, covered in a nutrient-dense goo, she undergoes a profound transformation, turning into a new form. Though the process is invisible to human eyes, she emerges as a butterfly with a completely new shape.

Similarly, grief transforms you in ways that may not be fully visible. Just as the butterfly's cells reorganize into her final form, your own emotional, physical, and spiritual landscapes are continually regenerating. Parts of you that feel dismantled will reorganize as you move with your emotions. The messy goo around you contains everything you need. Shed what no longer serves you and remain open to new possibilities. Through this process, maintain your connection with your beloved and be flexible with all the changes you're experiencing.

Just as lava cools to form new landforms, your anguish will eventually transform, allowing new awakenings and vitality to emerge.

Identify what you love most about these new months and find ways to invite those elements into your life. Whether it's the scent of earth after rain, the birds and their songs, or the beam of the sun or the moon, surround yourself with resonant joys.

March 1

The loss of a beloved companion is full of "firsts." Whether it's finding their first hair on your shirt, facing a holiday, or being asked about your beloved, each moment can feel overwhelming. It's okay to take a kindness pause for yourself and breathe deeply as you process it. Tune in to your body and emotions, allowing them to validate the difficulty of the moment as it passes.

♥ **INVITATION:** During a "firsts" moment, try saying out loud: *This is new. I honor the sadness that's moving through me.*

March 2

Invite beauty into your surroundings. Be intentional about what you choose to see and experience daily. These thoughtful choices can create a space that feels special and honors your beloved. Just as they brought beauty into your life, let the beauty around you now reflect the love and connection you share.

♥ **INVITATION:** Curate a small collection of pleasing items that remind you of your beloved and highlight them in the spaces you inhabit.

March 3

Every lesson your beloved left in your heart has shaped who you are today. Their legacy is like a seed planted deep within you, blossoming into acts of kindness, love, and compassion that you share with the world. Each time you choose empathy, kindness, or self-compassion, you honor their memory. Your beloved's spirit continues to guide you, inspiring you to live with love and purpose, reflecting the beauty they brought to your life.

♥ **INVITATION:** Choose one way you can honor their legacy today. How will you carry their spirit forward?

March 4

It's okay to select words that feel right when describing your beloved's experience. Some grieving guardians find words like "died" too harsh, preferring gentler terms like "left," "crossed over," "transitioned," or "passed away." Your word choices are personal and valid, and deserve to be honored.

♥ **INVITATION:** Write a list of words that do and don't resonate with you and notice how each one feels. Consider how you want to use these words to communicate authentically and in a way that supports you.

March 5

A powerful mission for you might be to help others. When you encounter someone who is struggling, worried, or tense, you can leap into action. With a deep breath in, welcome love, peace, and light. On the exhale, send nurturing, inspiring energy to that person. You can imagine bringing a smile of joy and wave of comfort to those around you who need it most.

♥ **INVITATION:** Say your beloved's name aloud and invite them in to collaborate with you by asking them for ideas on how to help someone. Listen for their response, which may arrive as an idea, an image, or a sound.

March 6

When your beloved transitions, everything can feel unsafe and unsteady because they provided you with a constant, unwavering love. Their presence was your sanctuary, offering unconditional acceptance and grounding you through life's ups and downs. This deep bond created a sense of stability that's irreplaceable. Their transition can make the world feel unfamiliar and unsettling as you adjust to this new reality.

♥ **INVITATION:** What's one small thing you can do today to find a sense of stability?

March 7

Expressing gratitude to our beloveds is more than just good manners; it's a path to discovery. Science shows that gratitude can positively impact our brain and heart, especially during grief. Every "thank you" whispered nurtures your heart and supports your healing. Gratitude helps us focus on the love and joy they brought and continue to bring, transforming grief into a celebration of their life.

♥ **INVITATION:** What "thank you" would you like to say to your beloved today?

March 8

Trees withstand even the worst storms because of their deep root systems. As you sway through difficult times, consider your own roots. What matters most to you? What principles guide your actions? When do you feel most aligned with who you truly are? Remember the deep roots that keep you connected to your true self.

♥ **INVITATION:** What's one action you can take today to reinforce a key part of your root system? For example, if compassion is one of your core roots, engage in an act of kindness for someone or an animal in need.

March 9

Don't waste another moment "waiting" instead of connecting! Waiting moments are often overlooked opportunities to hang out with your beloved. Next time you're in line or sitting in a waiting room, resist the urge to scroll through your phone. Instead, softly whisper your beloved's name and let your mind drift to a favorite memory. These simple acts transform mundane moments into meaningful reflections, keeping their spirit close.

♥ **INVITATION:** Next time you're waiting, connect with a memory. View this as treasured time you "get" to spend with them.

March 10

Your beloved's transition may feel like the heaviest burden you've ever carried. Just as your bond with them is unique, so too is your grief. Give yourself the patience and permission to grieve in your own way, without comparing it to any other loss. Just as every road has its own direction, this grief experience is solely yours—and that's perfectly okay.

♥ **INVITATION:** Write a commitment statement that begins, *I deserve…* focused on honoring what your distinctive grief experience truly deserves.

March 11

The power of a loving touch is immense. A soothing scalp massage can help you de-stress and reconnect with your body. Start by rubbing your palms together to generate warmth, then gently use your fingertips in circular motions, beginning at the front of your scalp and working your way back. Focus on your temples, the base of your skull, and the crown of your head. Even five minutes can offer a quick reset and endorphin release, bringing comfort and relaxation.

♥ **INVITATION:** Invite your beloved to join you in this soothing moment, sharing in the relaxation together.

March 12

Tarot and oracle card decks can be gentle, supportive tools during grief that you can use for reflection, self-discovery, and honoring your bond with your beloved. You don't need any special skills to start; tarot and oracle readings are simple and can be shaped around what feels right for you. It can offer you a safe place to explore your feelings without judgment.

♥ **INVITATION:** If you're interested, find a deck with artwork that resonates with you and begin by asking a simple question and drawing one card a day, using it as a moment to connect with your beloved and set a growth intention.

March 13

There's no medal or gold star for rushing through your grief. It isn't a race; it's a profound emotional, intellectual, and spiritual process that demands space, time, and your full attention. Instead of focusing on how long it's taking, consider what you're actively doing to participate in your grief. Remember, the pace is yours to set.

♥ **INVITATION:** What's one thing you can do today to support yourself more intentionally on this path?

March 14

When a beloved transitions, children often encounter loss for the first time. How you guide them through this experience shapes their understanding of grief. Honesty and emotional transparency are key—using clear, direct language helps children grasp what's happened and prevents confusion. Let them see your emotions and feel safe asking questions. This openness builds trust, supports their emotional growth, and models healthy mourning.

♥ **INVITATION:** Write out how you'll explain the transition and rehearse with another adult for confidence. Encourage children to express their feelings, creating a safe space for mutual sharing and connection.

March 15

Collect small stones, dedicating each one to a specific emotion that you are experiencing right now, then write or paint a symbol on each. Place these stones in a dish or on an altar. When one of these feelings arises, hold the corresponding stone, sitting with the emotion fully. As you breathe, in and out, feel the weight of the stone and imagine your emotion releasing into it. When you're ready, gently return the stone, allowing the feeling to flow through and leave you lighter. Thank the stone for helping you release your emotion.

♥ **INVITATION:** Write down how the release made you feel in your journal or a separate piece of paper.

March 16

Sometimes, well-meaning people may suggest welcoming another animal into your home before you're ready. This can feel like trying to patch a leak in your heart, overlooking the chasm of your grief. People often want to "fix" sadness, not realizing grief isn't something to be cured. Consider how you'd like to handle this comment, so you're not caught off guard.

♥ **INVITATION:** Practice this response if it resonates: *I appreciate your concern, but I'm not ready to welcome another family member yet. I'll let you know when or if that changes. Thanks for understanding.*

March 17

During grief, it's common to act in ways you're not proud of, such as snapping at loved ones, withdrawing, or saying things you don't mean. If that's happened to you, know you're not alone. What you're experiencing is incredibly challenging, and perfection isn't expected. It's okay to make amends, even if it's been a while. Apologies can help you move forward, restoring a sense of peace and connection with those you care about.

♥ **INVITATION:** Consider reaching out to someone today to apologize and take a meaningful and authentic step in your grief.

March 18

Sometimes it feels like everything stops. But you know what will never stop? You will never stop appreciating your beloved or stop feeling understood by them. You will never stop being rewarded by their memory, as flowers are rewarded with rain. You will never stop feeling wonder from their presence and learning from them. And you will never stop living your love story, which flows endlessly through your heart.

♥ **INVITATION:** Write your own list of things you will never stop doing with, for, and about your beloved. Read it aloud to your beloved for a moment of connection.

March 19

If you were not able to attend your beloved's transition and you're struggling with this, remember: you didn't plan or foresee this outcome. Not being physically present doesn't diminish the experience of love and care you shared. Your bond isn't defined by a single moment. Remember all the ways you nurtured them. They know how deeply you adore them.

♥ **INVITATION:** Write a letter to your beloved about what you wish you could have said if you had been present. Read it aloud so they can hear every word.

March 20

Nature often mirrors the duality we feel in grief, the darkness and the light ever changing and expanding. Even in darkness, new growth unfolds, consider how you might bloom within your grief. How can you be bold, assertive, or open, like the growing light around you? Let this balance guide you toward your next best step.

♥ **INVITATION:** Take an intentional walk to connect with your beloved or take time to get some fresh air. Notice the sights, sounds, and smells of the world around you. Take a moment to thank your beloved for sharing this moment of presence with you.

March 21

An unexpected side effect of grief is the sense that an entire chapter of your life has closed. When your beloved transitions, it often feels like more than just their absence—it feels like you're saying goodbye to a part of yourself. One supportive approach is to acknowledge that whole chapter of life where your beloved journeyed alongside you.

♥ **INVITATION:** List the pivotal moments, tough lows, and joyful times from this chapter. Acknowledge that you're not just mourning your beloved, you're mourning this entire era.

March 22

You are not "overreacting." Your grief needs—before, during, or after your beloved's transition—are not optional, and you're not asking too much to have them met. Whether it's feeling your feelings, taking time off work, talking with friends, seeking grief counseling, or anything else that feels right, you are reacting as you need to be, and you deserve to grieve fully and for as long as you need. Be loud, be messy, be unabashed. Your relationship with your beloved matters and so does your pain.

♥ **INVITATION:** Consider one way you've felt you are "overreacting" and rethink it through a lens of compassion. Then, say to yourself quietly or aloud: *I am not overreacting, I'm reacting to my grief.*

March 23

Supporting children through the loss of a beloved is a profound opportunity to teach them about death, adjustment, and celebrating a loved one. You're guiding them in how to grieve. Be honest, include them in the process, and answer every question. Remember, children comprehend loss differently at various ages and often grieve in spurts. Embrace rituals and traditions that honor their beloved. Above all, be patient as you help them navigate this difficult experience.

♥ **INVITATION:** Let children take the lead in memorial projects, such as funerals, crafts, scrapbooking, and writing in a family journal.

March 24

Your beloved offers a unique level of honesty that's unmatched by any other relationship. Their unconditional love and lack of judgment creates a safe space where you can be your truest self, free from the complexities often found in human relationships. This bond is rare and treasured, teaching you invaluable lessons about loyalty, affection, and authenticity. When faced with skepticism, remember that others may not fully understand the depth of this connection, but that doesn't diminish its truth.

♥ **INVITATION:** Remind yourself of a moment when your beloved's honesty made you feel truly seen. How did it impact you?

March 25

One of the loneliest parts of a beloved's transition is feeling like nobody sees your struggle. The barista making your coffee, the driver tailgating you; even close friends can seem oblivious to your pain. It's as if you're carrying a weight only you can feel. While this isolation may lessen as you adjust, for now, lean on people who truly understand. Confide in people who offer genuine support.

♥ **INVITATION:** Reach out to someone who has shown understanding. Share your feelings and remind yourself you're not alone.

March 26

Turning up the volume on parts of life that have been muted can bring relief. What areas can bolster your wellness? Consider relationships, fitness, nutrition, volunteer work, spirituality, hobbies, or self-care. Which of these can you do more of, or perhaps less of, as you navigate your sorrow? Like adjusting the dials on a radio, tuning in to what nurtures you most can help you find clarity and strength as you journey through your grief.

♥ **INVITATION:** Make a small, intentional shift that helps you raise the volume on what brings you reassurance and strength.

March 27

In their earthside life, you shared countless dreams and wishes with your beloved, creating a beautiful, intertwined love story. Every moment was a step toward realizing those shared visions, and together, you built a life filled with joy, adventure, and mutual care. Now that they've transitioned, it's time to check in with them again. Trust that their love and guidance continue to shine brightly, offering support and inspiration.

♥ **INVITATION:** Ask your beloved either out loud or in your head: *What do you hope for me? What are your dreams for my life?*

March 28

Nothing about grief is linear. Some days feel heavier than others, and it's okay to reset at any moment. Think of each day as a fresh start, like a sunrise after a stormy night. In grief, we face bad hours, bad days, and sometimes bad weeks, months, or years. Then, a reprieve comes, like a break in the clouds. A bad day doesn't mean you've backtracked. Tomorrow may bring something entirely different. Allow each day to unfold as it needs to, without judgment.

♥ **INVITATION:** Write a note to yourself for consolation during a "good" moment and one for courage during a "bad" moment.

March 29

Today, nurture yourself with the gift of a five-minute nature gaze. Find a subject you're drawn to, like a single flower, a patch of wild grass, a rippling pond, or a tree. Get comfortable and behold what's before you with genuine curiosity. Welcome this wonder into your world and allow this gentle moment of connection.

♥ **INVITATION:** Ask your beloved to experience this with you. Imagine the two of you taking it in together. What do they notice that you might not? What do you want to make sure they don't miss? Enjoy the conversation you share.

March 30

Caring for yourself during grief is like tuning a delicate instrument—one that plays the notes of the love you share with your beloved. The physical separation is painful, but the melody of your love continues, resonating deeply. At first, tuning in to this love may feel distant or murky, but don't give up. With patience, you'll hear the sweet harmony of your connection, guiding you as you move with your grief.

♥ **INVITATION:** What would be the titles of a track list about the album of the story of your life with your beloved?

March 31

We often feel like a chunk of our heart is missing, an unfillable and irreplaceable piece. When you notice that absence, imagine placing something powerful in that space. Close your eyes and envision what you'd like to hold there—maybe the face of your beloved, a rainbow, a crystal, a deity, or a fierce animal. Embody what it feels like to carry this power within you. What strength might you borrow to help you through the day?

♥ **INVITATION:** List sacred forces you'd like to invite into your heart. Each day, choose one with intention to become part of your support scaffolding.

April 1

Your body bears the weight of grief in unexpected ways. You might feel exhausted, tense, achy, agitated, or disconnected, as if carrying a heavy load. Because our minds and bodies are deeply intertwined, it's essential to give your body extra care. When heartache weighs on you, respond with love and kindness.

♥ **INVITATION:** Commit to one beneficial practice today: moving your body, spending time in nature, seeing a doctor, taking a warm bath, receiving a massage, or getting restorative sleep are good places to begin.

April 2

On milestone days (anniversaries, birthdays, or gotcha days), dedicating time to connect with your beloved can bring profound meaning. Engage in activities that uphold your bond, like visiting a favorite trail, writing a letter, creating a memorial, or decorating with their cherished items. Honoring them through acts of service can also keep their spirit alive—consider donating to a shelter, volunteering, or performing small acts of kindness in their name.

♥ **INVITATION:** Brainstorm the activities or acts of goodwill that make you feel closest to your beloved, and incorporate them into your next milestone day to honor their legacy.

April 3

In the 1990s, it was common for people to use pagers to send the code "143" to express "I love you." The numbers correspond to the number of letters in each word. Honor your beloved by adding the number of letters in their name to create a unique four-digit code in their memory. For example, if their name has five letters, your code becomes 1435.

♥ **INVITATION:** Write this signature number in the sand or snow, use it for lock combinations, and keep an eye out for this combo in the world as a way to connect.

April 4

You don't need to stay in pain to prove your commitment to your beloved. As your agony lifts, you might fear losing your connection. That's not the case. Releasing pain creates more room for the next chapter of your relationship to unfold. Less pain doesn't mean less love. Letting go doesn't weaken your bond; it allows it to grow in new, meaningful ways.

♥ **INVITATION:** Begin a journal entry with: *I release my pain to make room for...* and see where it goes.

April 5

Give yourself the gift of exploring what truly comforts you with your five senses. Do tropical beaches or mountains soothe your sight? Does the scent of peppermint or lavender lift your spirits? Do you crave the touch of fuzzy blankets? Prefer the sounds of a rainforest or a thunderstorm? Sour or sweet candies? When seeking comfort, engage all the five senses, weaving them into your self-care routine.

♥ **INVITATION:** Make a list of one thing you enjoy from each sense. Turn to it whenever you need a boost.

April 6

For centuries, mourning has been expressed through how we dress. You might reach for comforting clothes during this time, such as a well-worn sweater, a baseball cap with their name on it, or memorable jewelry. Wearing your animal's signature color or something that embodies their spirit can feel like wrapping yourself in their love.

♥ **INVITATION:** What's one way you can honor your beloved through clothing today? Incorporate it and notice how it feels to mourn through your fashion choice.

April 7

Caring for yourself during grief is like piloting a ship through uncharted waters, where each element requires careful navigation. Your physical health is the hull—keeping you afloat with regular meals, sleep, and exercise. Emotional well-being is the sail—catching the winds of your feelings and steering your course. Spiritual care is the compass—providing direction through reflection and meditation. Social connections are the crew—supporting you on your journey. Your relationship with your beloved is the North Star guiding you.

♥ **INVITATION:** Which part of your ship needs attention? What's one action you can take today to steady your course?

April 8

Self-forgiveness can soften the rough edges of regret and self-blame. Mistakes can be teachers, guiding us toward growth. Forgiveness is an open door, inviting you to be gentle with yourself. Embrace this chance to show yourself the kindness you give to others. You deserve it.

♥ **INVITATION:** Take a deep breath, place your hand over your heart, and acknowledge any mistakes or regrets without judgment. Then, gently tell yourself: *I forgive you. You were doing the best you could with the timing, knowledge, and love you had.*

April 9

The love between you and your beloved is boundless, effortless, measureless, and ceaseless. It's seamless, limitless, fearless, and endless. And even though they've transitioned from their earthly body, this love is not "less." Your relationship with your beloved continues, a sacred bond that transcends the physical. You honor this love each day, nurturing it as a source of strength and comfort, allowing it to guide you through your heartache.

❤ **INVITATION:** Make a word cloud with this prompt: *The love between my beloved and me is . . .*

April 10

You never have to move or donate your beloved's belongings if you're not ready. Their items are like cherished chapters in a book filled with memories and love that can't be replaced. Just as a book remains on the shelf until you're ready to revisit it, you can keep everything as it is for as long as you need. If your beloved's heirlooms bring you consolation, allow them to support you.

❤ **INVITATION:** Place one of your beloved's special items in a spot of honor in your home and give it a love boop each time you pass it.

April 11

Do you feel like everything has been taken away from you? That's a common and valid response. If you do, try to step back and consider what hasn't changed. You still have the power to choose your thoughts, to go for a walk and take in the beauty around you, or to talk with friends who care. You might not feel like doing these things now, but it's important to remind yourself that they're still there.

♥ **INVITATION:** Make a list of the things that haven't changed since the transition of your beloved.

April 12

It can be tough for anyone who cared for your beloved, such as their veterinarian, house sitter, groomer, or neighbor, as they grieve too. When you're ready, consider extending a thank-you note, photos, or an invitation to share memories. Acknowledging and honoring the grief of those who cared for your beloved can be a powerful way to express gratitude and find mutual support during this difficult time.

♥ **INVITATION:** Make a list of people who cared for your beloved and consider what offering might feel supportive to them as they mourn alongside you.

April 13

After your beloved transitions, it's natural for your mind to unravel with questions—*Did they know how much I loved them? Did I do enough?* These threads of doubt can pull you apart. Instead of focusing on what's missing, turn your attention to the glimmering threads of love you wove into your shared life. Self-compassion, acceptance, and remembering what you did for them are reminders to mend your heart.

❤ **INVITATION:** List the fun, cheesy, heartfelt ways you showed love to your beloved and keep it close for when doubts creep in.

April 14

Just as the moon moves through its phases, our grief shifts and evolves, each moment offering its own teachings. The new moon invites us to embrace darkness and set intentions. As the waxing crescent appears, we gently open to our emotions. The full moon urges us to confront and honor our deepest feelings. The waning gibbous provides space to release guilt and regret, while the waning crescent reminds us to rest and practice self-compassion.

❤ **INVITATION:** Which moon phase mirrors your grief today? How can you honor it?

April 15

Your beloved gave you the gift of unwavering connection and deep fulfillment. Their comfort, respect, and contentment were treasures beyond measure. Each day, they offered warmth and peace, making you feel that you belonged and were worthy just as you are. While you may never repay them, you can honor their memory by cherishing these gifts and continuing to create love.

♥ **INVITATION:** Choose one gift your beloved brought into your life and share it with someone in their honor.

April 16

Is gratitude even possible during grief? In a world where grief can feel like a thief, it's natural to resist finding gratitude when we feel so robbed. But gratitude is like a small flame in the darkness—it requires care and patience to nurture, especially when our pain feels all-consuming. If the thought of practicing gratitude feels too heavy right now, know that it's okay to set it aside or start with just a spark.

♥ **INVITATION:** Before you fall asleep, ask yourself: *What's one thing I am grateful for today?*

April 17

It can feel like you're waiting for a neon sign to light up, hoping your beloved's transition will reveal a greater truth that hasn't appeared yet. Trust that, in time, the messages you seek will come. If you focus too much on a big revelation, you might miss the small beams of wisdom each day offers. Allow your grief to evolve, knowing that deeper understanding will come when the time is right.

♥ **INVITATION:** When frustrated by uncertainty, place both hands over your heart and say: *I allow things to reveal themselves on their own time.*

April 18

Your beloved was there when you were down; when you felt hurt, rejected, imperfect, ashamed, stuck, unloved, and afraid. They saw you beyond how you saw yourself, offering mercy, joy, and compassion. As hard as it feels without their earthside presence, you can hold yourself in your grief as tenderly as they held you. Invite their love in once more, to cradle you in your mourning, just as they always did.

♥ **INVITATION:** If your beloved could whisper words of comfort right now, what would they say?

April 19

Showing up for your grief can feel like assembling a puzzle—each piece representing a different emotion that needs careful placement to reveal the bigger picture. Embracing your grief means not avoiding the difficult pieces but working through them to make space for other emotions—like courage, hope, and peace. Putting these pieces together is one of the most meaningful and empowering acts of self-compassion you can offer.

♥ **INVITATION**: Draw your grief as a puzzle. Name the pieces. What do you notice about the emotions that make up your grief? What's missing?

April 20

Sometimes, it feels easier to isolate than to talk about it. It feels safer to withdraw than to spend energy interacting. It feels kinder to retreat than to show how shattered you really are. Yet, while isolation might seem like a refuge, it can be a lonely place. Grief is often easier to carry with connection rather than solitude.

♥ **INVITATION**: Take a small step today—reach out to someone who understands, either online or in person, even if it's just a simple hello.

April 21

Want more connection with your beloved? Create time each day to tune in. Whether through meditation, lighting a candle, walking in nature, or writing to them, prioritize moments of deep, intentional connection. In these moments, feel their love, send love to them, and ask them to let you know they feel it. Ask them out loud for guidance or a sign. Try this daily and see what unfurls.

♥ **INVITATION:** What connection ritual will you begin today?

April 22

It's okay if you don't feel like looking on the bright side, thinking positively, or counting your blessings. The pressure to find silver linings can dismiss the depth of your pain. Your emotions are valid and deserve space to breathe. You don't have to seek a silver lining unless it feels right. Your grief deserves to be heard, expressed, and supported without needing to wrap it in a neat bow.

♥ **INVITATION:** If someone encourages you to "think more positively," remind yourself that you're allowed to feel a full range of emotions as you navigate your grief.

April 23

If you've always been good at nurturing your beloved and others, it might feel uncomfortable to receive care from yourself or others. Sometimes focusing on others allows us to avoid the vulnerability of acknowledging our own needs. Grief can be a powerful opportunity to start embracing vulnerability, both with yourself and those around you.

♥ **INVITATION:** Set a timer for sixty seconds and practice being gentle and loving with yourself. Speak to yourself with kindness and send warm, affirming thoughts your way.

April 24

Your beloved was your family, purpose, and connector. Your beloved was your catalyst, teacher, support—your everything. No wonder it hurts. A beloved's transition is heart-wrenching because they embody so many facets of love and companionship. The intensity of your grief reflects the depth of your bond. It's okay to feel this deeply—your love is profound and so is your anguish.

♥ **INVITATION:** Make a list of all the roles your beloved played in your life. What roles will they continue to play now?

April 25

Maybe you don't want to wash the towel from their transition, clean their paw prints, or remove their blanket from the car. Perhaps you sleep with their ashes or can't wipe their nose prints off the window. These actions aren't "weird." You're grieving your beloved, and there's no shame in treasuring these reminders. As long as they support you and aren't harmful, they're a soothing part of your process.

♥ **INVITATION:** Journal about what it would be like to mourn fully, openly, and completely as you want to—what would it look like?

April 26

The power of place to restore us during grief is often overlooked, especially when leaving home feels daunting. Think about a nature spot, nostalgic setting, or spiritual space that might offer support. Do you enjoy inhaling the scents in a spice shop, browsing the books in a bookstore or library, or exploring an art gallery? Seek surroundings that will nourish and uplift you during this time.

♥ **INVITATION:** List five locations you haven't visited recently that could support your grief, and invite your beloved along for an outing together.

April 27

Honor your beloved by sharing memories, much like revisiting the cherished pages of a well-loved photo album. Don't shy away from talking about them—keeping their story alive can bring comfort and connection. Social media is another space to celebrate your time together, offering a platform to tell the story of your life with your beloved, even amid deep grief. This act of remembrance can be profoundly enriching.

♥ **INVITATION:** Share a memory of your beloved once a week for the next three months.

April 28

It's common to feel stuck in your grief and it's easy to judge yourself when it happens. When you encounter a "stuck" moment, ask what you might be holding on to that's ready for release. What's keeping you from living in the present? It might be an old memory, self-criticism, or a behavior from early grief that has lingered too long.

♥ **INVITATION:** Imagine a bunch of balloons, each representing what's holding you back. Visualize releasing each one into the sky. Then say, *Thank you for your role in my life; I'm moving toward something wonderful now.*

April 29

Your love for your beloved doesn't end with their physical presence—it transforms. You can honor your beloved by keeping their memory close and extending that love to yourself. Redirect the compassion they gave you toward nurturing yourself. Grief becomes a journey of transformation, where the love you share guides you toward healing and growth.

♥ **INVITATION:** Repeat aloud or in writing: *I cherish and trust myself and remain open to receiving new avenues of love and care from myself and my beloved.*

April 30

When your beloved was earthside, you knew everything about them— their favorite activities, quirks, and deepest obsessions. After their transition, it feels lonely not knowing what they're doing or how they're feeling. Through your grief, aspire each day to become more comfortable with the unknowing and more assured in your continued love and connection.

♥ **INVITATION:** Take a quiet moment today to speak to your beloved, sharing your thoughts and inviting their presence into your heart. What message do you feel from them?

May 1

What can you *still* do in grief? You can still embrace your beloved. Close your eyes, feel their presence, and let the warmth of your memories enfold you. Revisit old photos or continue their favorite routines in their honor. Speak to them in quiet moments, sharing your day and your hopes, and feel their comforting presence in your heart's responses. Cherish every moment spent together and carry forward the love they gave you in acts of kindness to others.

♥ **INVITATION:** Ask yourself: *What can I still do and be for my beloved?* Write the answer in your journal.

May 2

When you long for the physical intimacy of your beloved, consider the soothing touch of a cozy object. Depending on your beloved's size, a heated rice pillow, bean bag stuffed animal, or weighted blanket rolled into an approximate shape might feel supportive. Your heart and brain miss the physical presence of your beloved and it's often supportive to have a warm comfort that reminds us of their form.

♥ **INVITATION:** Draw a picture of your body and mark hearts around all the places your beloved regularly touched, nuzzled, or snuggled up to. Then, experiment with weighted objects on those spaces for support.

May 3

Your grieving experience doesn't need to only be full of sorrow. Laughter is allowed. Joking is allowed. Singing loudly and off-key is allowed. Smiling releases endorphins that soothe pain, neuropeptides that relieve stress, and serotonin that acts as an antidepressant. When humor finds its way to you during grief, welcome and embrace the relief. Laughter is a key element of your bond with your soulmate. Allow it to continue as part of your beloved's legacy in the world.

❤ **INVITATION:** Think of a time when your beloved made you giddy and write the whole story.

May 4

Welcoming a new relationship into your family—whether human or animal—doesn't mean you're "over" your grief. Your unique bond with your beloved can never be replaced. You're allowed to grieve your soulmate while feeling joy for this new addition. Through stories and memories, you can introduce them to each other, creating a thoughtful connection that honors both. This ritual can enrich your family's narrative and keep your beloved's spirit close.

❤ **INVITATION:** Write down the top ten "must-tell" stories about your beloved that you want to ensure remain a part of your family's lore. Consider creative ways to share or celebrate these stories.

May 5

Create an altar that honors your beloved animal. Assemble a collection of meaningful items and photos in an area that feels calm and safe to you. Every time you pass it by, speak words of love. Clean and rearrange your altar each week, tending to it as you have always tended to your beloved. Allow it to be a place of reverie, respect, and rejuvenation.

❤ **INVITATION:** Refresh your beloved's altar with treats, flowers, or decorations for the seasons.

May 6

Find a quiet space and begin with a simple hum or melody that resonates with your emotions—whether it's sadness, anger, or longing. Feel the vibrations in your chest and throat, allowing the sound to express your grief. Let the melody flow, tuning in to what it's trying to communicate. As you relax into the sound, ask yourself: *Where have I shown resilience lately? What within me has inspired others? How do I bring light? Where can I honor my growth?*

❤ **INVITATION:** Choose a song or melody that reflects your current emotions. Sing or hum it each day for a week, noticing how this practice impacts your feelings.

May 7

What needs encouraging today? Perhaps openness, deep listening, gratitude, or connection with your beloved? Today, act in alignment with an intention you set, observing your interactions with yourself and with others. Congratulate yourself when you meet your intention. Be kind to yourself for the moments you're not in alignment with your intention—this practice may take some time to feel comfortable—and give your grief the gift of focused intention each day.

♥ **INVITATION:** Set an intention at the start of each day this week

May 8

Lighting a candle in honor of your beloved at significant times of the day can foster deeper connection. If there's a sacred time of the day for you, whether that's walk time, play time, medicine time, or food time, it might feel supportive to light a candle and whisper a few words of love to your beloved. Taking a moment to breathe, slow down, invite in your love, and listen to what comes can make a soothing reset for your day.

♥ **INVITATION:** If it feels right, you might choose a personalized name or photo candle to honor your beloved.

May 9

It's common to feel unseen as we mourn. Even well-meaning people can make us feel invisible in our sorrow when they avoid the topic of our loss, which amplifies feelings of isolation. When this happens, remind yourself that many people are uncomfortable with grief, and they may worry about saying the wrong thing or believe that they are sparing you discomfort by not mentioning it.

♥ **INVITATION:** Let someone know that you welcome their support and that you are open to discussing your grief.

May 10

Are you a self-proclaimed perfectionist? If so, it's impacting your grief. Perfectionism, like a suit of armor, shields us from fears of not being enough or disappointing others. But grief isn't something you can perfect—it's disorderly and fickle. Trying to grieve perfectly is impossible, and it's okay to let that armor down and allow yourself to feel what you need to feel.

♥ **INVITATION:** Today, choose one thing about yourself you would like to embrace rather than "fix." What will it be?

May 11

If you relate to your beloved as a mom, Mother's Day can feel thorny, especially if people forget to acknowledge your role. If you're struggling with this on Mother's Day, know your role as mom is recognized. Remember, societal norms often overlook the profound connection between animal parents and their non-human children. You're still your beloved's mom. Your place as your beloved's mom will never end.

♥ **INVITATION:** Write a Mother's Day card to yourself in the voice of your beloved. What gratitude do they want to share with you about you?

May 12

We all wish we could have stopped any bad thing from happening to our beloveds, even their transitions. It can feel scary and powerless to not have control over accidents, medical events, and the aging process. Sometimes we assume fault and blame when the circumstances may have been beyond our power to control.

♥ **INVITATION:** If you notice you're being hard on yourself because you couldn't control the outcome of your beloved's situation, remind yourself, *I wish it had been different for my beloved, but that doesn't make it my fault.*

May 13

You are like a leaf, connected to a strong tree. Just as a leaf bends in the wind, you too can be flexible and resilient. Your emotional veins support you, helping you adapt, change, and move with grace. You are grounded, connected, and resilient.

♥ **INVITATION:** Repeat to yourself silently or aloud: *Today, I move with my grief like a leaf in the wind.*

May 14

In many ancient cultures, tattoos were used to honor ancestors in mourning rituals. Custom tattoos, whether temporary or permanent, can serve as beautiful reminders of your beloved in daily life. Detailed portraits, the coordinates where you first met, special phrases, significant symbols, paw prints, and names can all be powerful expressions of connection. You might even choose to incorporate some of your beloved's remains into the ink. If this doesn't feel right to you, consider a painting as an alternative.

♥ **INVITATION:** List symbols, words, and imagery for a potential memorial tattoo. Do any strike you as ink-worthy?

May 15

Anger is often a "cover story" for other emotions, such as unmet needs, expectations, or hurt. When anger arises, it can be helpful to check in with yourself and explore what else you might be feeling. Acknowledging statements like, "I feel hurt right now," or "I honor my unmet expectations about my life with my beloved," can diffuse anger and nurture you.

❤ **INVITATION:** Draw your anger as a shield. Inside the shield, write or draw all the emotions that may be hiding beneath your anger.

May 16

Moving while grieving your beloved can feel like packing up your heart and leaving pieces behind. It's natural to experience a mix of emotions. If a move is in your future, consider a closing ritual in your old space to honor your bond. Don't rush to part with their belongings; bring them along if it feels right. In your new home, create a sacred space for a tribute.

❤ **INVITATION:** Plan how to move your beloved's sacred possessions. Would creating their space first in your new home help you feel more connected and supported?

May 17

Take a quiet moment to tune in to your body, noticing any sensations—tightness in your chest, heaviness in your stomach, or tension in your shoulders. Gently ask: *What might my body be telling me about my grief?* Our bodies often retain the emotions we can't yet name. Notice if something feels difficult—like making eye contact or sitting still. Could this be connected to guilt, sadness, or another layer of grief your body is holding?

♥ **INVITATION:** Gently scan your body. Where are you clutching grief? Choose how you can honor and extricate these feelings today.

May 18

You may find that crying isn't your go-to expression or that, over time, you cry less or for different reasons. If you're not crying often, it doesn't mean you're any less affected or that your relationship with your beloved is less meaningful. Crying is just one form of release and it's okay if other expressions feel more supportive. Be kind to yourself by releasing any judgment about crying—it's not a measure of your love.

♥ **INVITATION:** Say this to yourself quietly or aloud: *Today, I will not judge my grief expressions and will express my grief fully and freely.*

May 19

You're not being lazy; you're grieving. Grief is devastating, leaving you physically, mentally, and emotionally drained. Your energy has been obliterated. You may feel like you're not doing enough because you're constantly tired, but that's what grief often looks like. Meet your obligations but give yourself permission to rest. Just as nature takes time to recover after a storm, you too need time to heal. Allow yourself the rejuvenation you deserve.

♥ **INVITATION:** Create a cozy space in your home for rest to explore naps, quiet reflections, or simply sitting.

May 20

Taking time off to mourn your beloved is essential, even if your workplace doesn't recognize animal grief. Your sadness deserves space and time. If stepping away isn't possible, try carving out dedicated moments for yourself within your constraints. Your well-being is paramount, and it's okay to say, "I need a moment," and nurture your hurt. Prioritizing your emotional health is crucial in honoring the love and bond you share.

♥ **INVITATION:** Brainstorm ways to adjust your work routine to create more space for mourning. If you have a supportive coworker, see if they can hold space for you right now.

May 21

"Grief brain" is a challenging and frustrating symptom of deep grief, causing real discomfort in your mind—you may feel spacey, tired, distracted, forgetful, and find tasks challenging. Everyone's timeline for improvement is unique. While there's no certainty for when it will get better, being gentle with yourself is crucial.

♥ **INVITATION:** When you notice a hazy moment, offer your brain some kindness for what it's experiencing and allow it to drift as it needs. Acknowledging your brain's need to not be 100 percent is supportive and loving.

May 22

The transition of your beloved often pushes you—willingly or not—into a new self-identity. And sometimes, this brings unexpected gifts. You might discover greater self-acceptance, stronger boundaries, or a newfound resolve to stand up for yourself, like a river carving out a new path after a heavy rain.

♥ **INVITATION:** List ways your self-identity has shifted for the better since your beloved's transition.

May 23

Create a legacy project, such as providing a box of tennis balls at a dog park, baking treats for a veterinary clinic, or bringing cozy sweaters to shelter animals. These offerings are heartfelt ways to honor your beloved's memory while spreading warmth and kindness in their wonderful name.

♥ **INVITATION:** When you create a legacy project, consider adding a sign or sticker with your beloved's picture and name, letting others know the beautiful soul behind this act of love.

May 24

Sometimes, answering a single email feels as if you've climbed a mountain. Taking a shower or eating a meal might be your biggest victory of the day. Don't diminish these wins, no matter how small they seem. In the fog of bereavement, every step forward is a triumph, like finding a small light in the darkness. Your best, no matter how modest, is enough. Honor every effort you make.

♥ **INVITATION:** Start a list of "grief wins" for you to return to when you are having a low moment.

May 25

It's common to worry that your grief might make you a "downer" to family and friends. You might feel like a dimmed light in a room of brightness, struggling to be your usual self. But remember, you're grieving, and that's a natural part of life's cycle. Just as a flickering candle still provides warmth and light, your presence, even in grief, is valuable and meaningful to those who love you.

❤ **INVITATION:** Embrace your emotions, communicate honestly, and set boundaries. Allow your grief to flicker and spark, trusting that being authentic is the most supportive path for healing.

May 26

If you had only six words to capture your beloved's most impactful life lesson, what would they be? Your beloved's wisdom, care, and deep understanding of your well-being held profound lessons. What do you discover when you distill all that into six powerful words?

❤ **INVITATION:** Write down this impactful lesson and place it somewhere visible—on your refrigerator, inside your medicine cabinet, or in your car—to remind you of their love and strength as you navigate your day.

May 27

Grieving your beloved is like walking through a dense forest—there is no straight path, and the journey unfolds at its own pace. Some might urge you to "move on," or you might think the same in frustration. But just as each forest has its own terrain, your grief is as unique as the bond you share. Take the time you need to navigate this immense shift.

♥ **INVITATION:** Imagine the forest of your grief—what do you see? Draw it, capturing the textures, paths, and shadows of your journey.

May 28

Imagine basking in the warmth of the sun, letting it fill you up with the same comfort your beloved brought into your life. Taking in the sun's rays can help you radiate kindness and openness as you move through your day. By absorbing the sun's energy and sharing it with others, you create a loving legacy of warmth, just as your beloved did.

♥ **INVITATION:** Enjoy a five-minute sun bath, then offer one act of warmth to your community, using your beloved and the sun as your inspiration.

May 29

Find a quiet space and sit with a bowl of water in front of you. Take a deep breath and set an intention to focus on one loud emotion you wish to release—perhaps anger, guilt, or sadness. Place your hands around the bowl, feeling the coolness of the water. Visualize energy flowing from your heart, through your arms, and into the water, letting it absorb and hold this emotion fully. Allow the water to be a container for this intense feeling, giving it a place to exist outside of you.

♥ **INVITATION:** Decide how to transmute this energy. Boil the water to spread it for cleansing, release it into nature, freeze and shatter it, or simply hold it in quiet reflection.

May 30

You may feel like you're on a roller coaster with no end in sight—one moment coasting, the next, plunging into deep emotional lows. It's no surprise that some days feel unbearable while others are more manageable. This emotional whiplash is a common part of grieving. Remember, these fluctuating feelings are typical and part of your unique experience.

♥ **INVITATION:** Remember past highs and lows. What helped you weather those? How can that wisdom bolster you now?

May 31

If it's not supportive to spend time with people who are dismissive of your experience, skip it. You're not obligated to explain your sadness. If it doesn't feel supportive to do certain traditions the same this year, don't. It's okay to feel overwhelmed and nostalgic.

❤ **INVITATION:** Make a list of three things you'd like to do this season in honor of your beloved.

Traditions and gatherings that once felt effortless might now seem challenging as you grieve. These times may highlight what's missing: your beloved's earthside presence. During times of celebration, you may feel left out or alone. As you build resilience in learning to tolerate your beloved's physical absence, you can still include and celebrate with them.

During a gathering, create a moment for communal reflection and connection. Organize a sharing circle or memorial to celebrate your beloved's life with friends and family. Through storytelling, activity, and shared memories, live their legacy and welcome unity and abundance. This is just one way that you can still celebrate and revere your beloved.

During these months, you want to make sure you are also caring for yourself and actively cultivating abundance into your life. Engage your inner child, who may crave play, spontaneity, and nostalgic comforts. Add some playful activities to your routine in praise of your beloved, such as flying kites, blowing bubbles, sketching chalk-drawing portraits, enjoying a popsicle, or having a picnic at the park. These joyful activities help nurture your connection to your beloved and to the child within you.

As you journey through your healing, appreciate the vibrancy your beloved brought (and still brings) into your life. Praise their life and celebrate the joy they provided.

June 1

As you contemplate the earthside time you spent with your beloved, it's natural to feel a deep sense of loss for the future you imagined together and all the things you desired to do, be, and see with them. Those plans may no longer feel possible, but your ability to collaborate remains.

♥ **INVITATION:** Write down a wish or plan you had with your beloved that feels out of reach. Then, brainstorm a new way to honor that dream. It might be volunteering, creating art, or starting a new learning or self-care practice.

June 2

Use the grief feelings wheel on page 221 as a loving daily check-in with yourself. Choose an emotion that feels the loudest in this moment and place your finger on it. Close your eyes, take a deep breath, and consider how this word resonates with your grief. What does this feeling need to be supported?

♥ **INVITATION:** Choose a small action based on the chosen emotion. For "sadness," perhaps allow yourself extra rest; for "hope," take a walk. Let this be a kind daily check-in.

June 3

Try emphasizing the present. One day, one hour, or even one breath at a time. Just for today, be gentle with yourself. Just for this hour, find the courage to face your feelings. Just for this minute, be fully present. And just for this second, honor your breath.

♥ **INVITATION:** Take a moment now to focus on your respiration and ground yourself in the present.

June 4

Engaging in creative activities like crafting a photo collage, writing poetry, or creating a vision board allows you to channel your devotion into something tangible and beautiful. These expressions become lasting tributes, saluting both your beloved's impact and your mourning. Creativity bridges your internal reflections with the external world and makes your inner thoughts visible.

💜 **INVITATION:** Choose a project that resonates with you and create it with togetherness in mind. Consider sharing it with someone who understands your feelings.

June 5

Sit quietly and envision the light that your beloved brought into your life. Let this radiance fill your heart. This illumination, nurtured by the love you share, remains a guiding beacon as you trek through life. Embrace this light that honors the special bond that still lives within you.

💜 **INVITATION:** Write down how this radiance continues to encompass you, especially during challenging moments. Revisit these words whenever you need to feel guided.

June 6

Our expressions are based on many dimensions and can often look starkly different for everyone, which can sometimes lead to misunderstandings. Being aware that different grief styles exist, especially when others around you are also grieving, is crucial. Effective communication and expressing needs clearly can support everyone involved.

♥ **INVITATION:** Discuss with someone who is grieving alongside you what support they need and share your own needs as well. Explore how you can honor your different grief styles together.

June 7

How do you view your grief? As an intruder, a threat, or a typhoon? A chatty relative you're forced to sit next to at a family holiday celebration? Instead, what if grief were a friend walking beside you? It might be a friend with opposing wants and needs or one who pushes boundaries, but it could also be a companion, offering solace, clarity, and new perspectives. Adjusting how you perceive your grief might bring deeper understanding.

♥ **INVITATION:** Write a letter to your grief, describing what you know about it and how you envision it to be. If it feels supportive, consider personifying your grief and allow it to write a letter back to you.

June 8

How has your beloved's presence changed since their transition? Perhaps they felt like a partner, while earthside, and now more like a protector. Or maybe they seemed like a child before and now feel like a guiding spirit. As their presence evolves, welcome it and allow for the possibilities your new connection offers.

♥ **INVITATION:** Write about your beloved's earthside presence and imagine how your connection might continue to mature in this new phase of life together.

June 9

Navigating social situations while grieving can be challenging. Prepare concise phrases to express your feelings without oversharing. For example, you can say, *It's been tough*, or *I'm taking it day by day*. This strategy helps you stay authentic while maintaining emotional boundaries.

♥ **INVITATION:** Write down your go-to phrases and keep them handy on an index card or in your phone. This preparation will make you feel more equipped during difficult conversations, enabling you to share as much or as little as you wish.

June 10

What activities motivate you? What hobbies soothe your spirit? What rejuvenates your mind, replenishes your body, or caresses your heart? These are your stepping stones, helping you cross grief's rapid-filled river. Identifying concrete things that bring you pleasure, stimulation, and ease creates a path you can follow when the currents feel overwhelming.

♥ **INVITATION:** Start a "pleasure list" of stepping stones you can turn to for a boost. You might also keep a "not-pleasure" list to remind yourself of what drains you, encouraging you to invite less of those into your daily life.

June 11

Claude Monet was so captivated by water lilies that he painted at least 250 of them, each capturing a unique nuance. Similarly to the way we often marveled at our beloveds—how they navigated the world, engaged with it, defied norms, and loved fiercely. These qualities can continue to inspire you, even after their transition.

♥ **INVITATION:** Make a list of what you admire most about your beloved. Then, explore how you can deepen your reverence by actively manifesting those qualities in your actions today.

June 12

Finding community during heartache can be like uncovering a hidden cave full of radiant crystals—suddenly seeing vibrant color when the world feels grey. While solitude may feel protective, connecting with people who truly understand can soothe your core. Speaking your truth and hearing the truths of others can be empowering when hope seems far away.

♥ **INVITATION:** Reach out to a community or person to share your grief with and allow their caring to brighten your journey.

June 13

Your "to-do" list might feel endless—sorting through medical bills, notifying care providers, deciding what to do with belongings, keeping up with your work and family pressures, and even rekindling relationships that may have faltered during your anticipatory grief or the aftermath of your beloved's transition. The strain is real, and it's okay to feel that weight. Amid all of this, finding a safe retreat where you can momentarily escape the pressure is crucial.

♥ **INVITATION:** Take a moment today to identify where you feel most at peace. Make time to visit that place and allow yourself to breathe.

June 14

If you're angry at the universe because your beloved transitioned, know that your feelings of being robbed are valid. But consider this: If the universe "took" your beloved, isn't it the same universe that brought you together? Think of all the tiny dominos that had to fall for you to find each other and embark on life in tandem. What an incredible series of events led your two souls together.

❤ **INVITATION:** When anger at the universe arises, say this out loud or quietly: *Thank you, universe, for helping our spirits meet. I'm so grateful we found each other.*

June 15

Your surviving animals also grieve. Many guardians observe behaviors like searching, lingering in favorite spots, or even taking on the traits of a transitioned beloved. Even if their suffering isn't visible, acknowledging it is vital. Speak to your surviving animals about what's happening and offer them extra comfort and reassurance. Engaging them in your mourning creates a mutual support system and strengthens your bond.

❤ **INVITATION:** How can you create new, comforting routines with your surviving animal(s) that keep them included in your mourning and honoring your beloved?

June 16

Have you noticed your posture slumping? Bereavement can physically weigh us down, making us want to shrink and hide. But what if you tried something different? Lift your head, roll your shoulders back, and stand tall with dignity and grace. Allow yourself to be seen in your grief, embodying both power and heartache.

♥ **INVITATION:** Take a moment today to adjust your posture. How does it change your feelings?

June 17

Your beloved's perseverance and tenacity were remarkable. Like a hidden spring quietly nourishing the land, their courage sustained them through every challenge. Now, as you face your own difficulties, draw from that same well of resilience.

♥ **INVITATION:** Journal about the lessons of fortitude your beloved demonstrated and how they've inspired you. Let their hidden spring of strength be a well you return to whenever you need support.

June 18

Kind phrases are powerful wishes we offer ourselves to nurture our hearts. Begin with these three questions: *What do I need to hear from the universe? What do I need to hear from my community? What do I need to hear from my beloved?* These questions guide us to create affirmations that address our needs for safety, connection, and strength.

♥ **INVITATION:** Create three loving-kindness phrases to repeat each morning and night. Examples might be, *May I be safe, May I know my strength,* or *May I feel connected to my beloved.*

June 19

Decluttering your physical space can declutter your mind, creating paths for new energy and fresh perspectives. In grief, certain objects or rooms may feel overwhelming. By reorganizing or letting go of items that no longer serve you, you make space for healing and for what truly brings solace and cheer.

♥ **INVITATION:** Take time today to declutter a small space, such as a drawer, shelf, or corner that feels heavy. Afterward, spend a few moments breathing in the reinvigorated environment you've created.

June 20

Take a moment to acknowledge the weight of "masking"—feeling like you have to be "on" for others while carrying heaviness inside. Breathe deeply and allow yourself to release the pressure to present a certain way. Visualize removing a mask, one that holds your efforts to appear "okay." Imagine setting it down and letting your authentic emotions breathe. Remind yourself it's acceptable to not have it all together.

♥ **INVITATION:** Find a comfortable spot, close your eyes, and practice gentle self-massage on your hands, arms, or shoulders. Allow this touch to be a reminder that you deserve care, even when you're holding back emotions.

June 21

Imagining a reunion with your beloved can be a comforting thought even if you're unsure of what lies beyond. Visualizing a peaceful place where your beloved awaits might provide solace. Whether it's a belief, a dream, or simply a hope, envisioning your beloved with other important ancestors or wishing for a reunion can be a stabilizing comfort.

♥ **INVITATION:** Write a dialogue between you and your beloved for when that reunion day finally comes.

June 22

Just as food nourishes or hinders your body, what you feed your mind can either uplift or burden your spirit. Recognize if you're absorbing unnecessary tragedy, despair, or helplessness. Negativity can distress you during grief, even if it didn't before.

♥ **INVITATION:** Evaluate what you're serving your mind. Set boundaries, unfollow upsetting social media accounts, or create a new, separate profile dedicated to content that inspires and warms your spirit.

June 23

Create a small, private gesture just for you and your beloved that symbolizes your ongoing love story. Choose a spot on your body where you can discreetly pat, clasp, or touch—perhaps a gentle squeeze of a finger or a tap on your wrist. This subtle action can offer a comforting connection whenever you need it.

♥ **INVITATION:** Draw a heart, paw, or initial in your beloved's signature color on your body to create a visual place to touch.

June 24

Grief can amplify emotions, making them feel flailing and urgent. This might lead to immediate reactions without much thought. Remember, you have options. By pausing and asking yourself: *How do I want to respond to this?* you create space for more intentional and compassionate choices. This practice helps you navigate your grief with greater mindfulness.

♥ **INVITATION:** Next time you experience a strong emotion, take a pause to choose your response before reacting and acting on that emotion.

June 25

You now carry a unique wisdom—one you never asked for, but it's become part of you. Like rare gems uncovered deep within the earth, this knowledge has been shaped by intense pressure and time, offering clarity and value to those just beginning their journey. When you're ready, consider how you might use these gems to guide and support others.

♥ **INVITATION:** If you were writing a letter to a new grieving guardian, what advice and encouragements would you offer them?

June 26

Are there bits of reassurance that you can almost hear your beloved saying—words that resonate within your soul? Words can be like a soft breeze, uplifting you when the weight of grief feels too much to bear. Curate a collection of these comforting phrases to depend on whenever you need an extra boost.

♥ **INVITATION:** Write uplifting quotes or reminders on slips of paper in your beloved's signature color and place them in a basket or jar. Whenever you need a pep talk, draw one out and let their insight inspire you.

June 27

Think about the strengths within your support network. Some friends plan thrilling outings while others excel at practical tasks like cooking or folding laundry. Perhaps a buddy of your beloved would enjoy illustrating a custom paint-by-number with you or crafting a scrapbook. Recognizing each person's unique abilities and capacities allows you to seek support that truly meets your needs and provides opportunities for your loved one to shine.

♥ **INVITATION:** Identify the attributes of your village and request the specific care you desire, whether it's a fun distraction, logistical help, or a listening ear.

June 28

Traveling can feel like stepping into a fresh current, sweeping you into a new environment that revives your spirit and strengthens your bond. Whether revisiting a meaningful place or exploring somewhere new, leaving your usual surroundings offers fresh perspectives and a renewed sense of connection. These journeys, however brief, can serve as both a homage and a way to restore yourself.

❤ **INVITATION:** Plan a visit to a special place—whether it's a favorite park, a cherished spot your beloved loved, or somewhere new. Embrace the memories and emotions it evokes.

June 29

Even if prayer feels unfamiliar to you or your beliefs are uncertain, experimenting with prayer writing can still be meaningful. Dedicate a moment each day to speak a devotion—whether to yourself, your beloved, or the universe—and notice how it anchors and connects you.

❤ **INVITATION:** Write a prayer that reflects your feelings. If you're not sure where to begin, you could try asking yourself what you hope to feel, receive, or share in this moment. Or simply start by sending love or gratitude in words—to yourself, your beloved, or the universe. Notice how creating and speaking this prayer affects you.

June 30

When intrusive, guilty, or upsetting thoughts appear, your mind might be trying to make sense of your experience. Rather than pushing the negative thoughts away, try gently releasing or acknowledging them. Doing this can be effective in managing intense thoughts.

♥ **INVITATION:** When a disruptive thought appears, say aloud: *No thank you. That does not feel supportive to me right now,* or acknowledge it with: *I see you. I hear you. I know you're trying to get my attention. You are welcome here and can stay as long as you need.*

115

JUNE

July 1

Try activating awe as a glimmer that awakens your energy. Awe is like a sparkler that lights up the darkness, giving you glimpses of hope and strength. Think back to the last time you felt true reverence—where were you? What was it like? Who was there? How can you recreate it? Are there lyrics, art, music, or natural wonders that fill you with astonishment?

♥ **INVITATION:** Make a date on your calendar for an awe-inspiring experience.

July 2

It's natural to seek escape through food, alcohol, or other momentary distractions. Yet, these methods won't erase misery and may intensify your emotions. Experience your feelings fully without suppressing them. Let your grief outpourings be genuine, giving your instincts the space they need to be perceived. This approach helps you move with the pain rather than getting stuck in it.

♥ **INVITATION:** How are you coping? What healthier strategies can you adopt when you feel the urge to numb or evade your pain?

July 3

If you're speaking unkindly to yourself during your grief, you're piling suffering onto the distress you're already carrying. Self-kindness is essential. You're navigating deep sorrow, and mean inner dialogue only adds to the burden. Your beloved would never speak to you as harshly as you do. Offer yourself the same grace, empathy, and nurturing that your beloved would grant you.

♥ **INVITATION:** When you need support, say these loving phrases to yourself: *This is hard. It's okay that I'm struggling. I am doing my best.*

July 4

You may expect to miss your beloved during tough times, but grief can also surprise you during occasions of satisfaction and triumph. These moments can feel bittersweet as you realize they aren't there to rejoice with you. This is understandable as they were your partner in all things and their earthside absence is felt deeply.

♥ **INVITATION:** Plan ways to include your beloved in upcoming celebratory instances. And when an unexpected jolt of elation occurs, let your beloved be the first one to hear the terrific news.

July 5

Grief is a tremendous revealer of limitations in others. Seeking support from people who don't get it is like going to purchase milk at the hardware store. Some may feel intimidated by your sadness and tears, wanting to "resolve" it due to their own discomfort. While this can be difficult, aim to extend grace when others fall short. If someone close missteps during your grief, consider clearing the air when you're ready. Grief challenges everyone, and what people say is not always personal.

♥ **INVITATION:** Write any unresolved feelings between you and someone you care about and consider initiating a heartfelt conversation.

July 6

Enduring envy, resentment, or blame can expose important lessons. Instead of dismissing these emotions, ask: *Who do I want to be in this resentment? Does blame reflect who I strive to become?* Consider if these feelings align with who your beloved inspires you to be. When ready, you may choose to release some of this weight and start healing.

♥ **INVITATION:** Free-write about how these emotions are impacting you. Is there a part of your grief you're ready to liberate? How will you begin?

July 7

Contemplate the teachings your beloved instilled in you—serenity, fulfillment in simple things, presence, boundaries, or unconditional love. These meaningful principles continue to empower who you are. How did your beloved gently motivate you to learn new things?

♥ **INVITATION:** Teach someone else a lesson you learned from your beloved. Whether it's sharing the satisfaction of a simple walk or demonstrating the value of patience, distribute these gifts and keep their wisdom alive by sharing them with others.

July 8

It's not betrayal to feel relief when your beloved dies, especially after enduring a tough diagnosis or caregiving period. It's not disloyal to feel grateful that their suffering has ended. Feeling anger or blame toward them is also common, even if they didn't choose to leave. Grief stirs a complex brew of emotions, and each one of them is reasonable.

♥ **INVITATION:** Say this aloud or write it down: *I cannot betray my beloved by feeling or thinking something. My beloved is safe. Our connection remains strong.*

July 9

A beloved's transition at a young age brings a unique depth of pain. It's like a song ending mid-note, leaving a hollow hush. You may struggle with unfulfilled hopes, compare your experience to others, feel jealousy and anger, and question your spiritual beliefs. The reactions of others can add to the hurt. Your emotions are like the steady beat of a drum— persistent, resonant, and deserving of being heard.

♥ **INVITATION:** Write down your complex feelings about how young your beloved was when they transitioned, honoring each one as it reverberates.

July 10

Recall the peaceful end-of-day rituals you shared when your beloved was earthside, like the closing of a favorite chapter, where each night brought solace and a sense of ease. These routines were a gentle affirmation of your connection, offering a moment of soothing together before sleep.

♥ **INVITATION:** Start a new nightly ritual with your beloved. You could begin with reading aloud stories, poems, or childhood books you love.

July 11

Not publicly announcing your beloved's transition doesn't diminish your relationship. You decide what, when, and how to convey, if ever, anything about their completion of life. Feedback will follow, which can be challenging to process, so trust your heart to guide the timing of your disclosures.

❤ **INVITATION:** What is the difference between secrecy and privacy? What did you learn about these concepts growing up? Discerning these distinctions can help relieve the pressure to provide details before you're ready.

July 12

Grieving the transition of your beloved also means grieving the loss of the person you were before. Missing who you used to be before is common. You're not the same and that's okay. As you mourn, allow yourself to mourn the parts of you that have changed. Recognize the transformation within you and give yourself the space to grieve what won't reconstitute.

❤ **INVITATION:** Write down the parts of your pre-loss self that you can emancipate to welcome who you are now and consider how this revision has reconfigured you.

July 13

Think about all the nicknames you showered on your beloved—each one a quirky, loving nugget rooted in observation and hilarity. These names capture their essence and the bond between you, evolving over time like a secret language only you two understand. Revisiting them can be a whimsical romp down memory lane, guaranteed to brighten any gloomy day.

♥ **INVITATION:** Create a catalog of these endearing nicknames and delight in their significance. Each one is a playful reminder of the intimacy you share and the connection that endures.

July 14

If you chose not to attend your beloved's euthanasia, grant yourself the peace you deserve. While being present during those final moments can be meaningful, it can also be unbearable for some. If your presence might have added distress for you, your beloved, or the veterinary staff, your decision to retreat was both kind and wise. Your love isn't defined by that single moment but by the deep devotion and countless memories you share.

♥ **INVITATION:** Remind yourself of the love and memories you created throughout your beloved's life. Write down three moments that capture the depth of your affection and adoration.

July 15

Find a quiet space and use the grief feelings wheel on page 221 to identify an intense emotion that you are struggling with. Write it down. Think about the soft words you would offer a loved one experiencing this. Speak these words aloud to yourself, letting each phrase land softly.

♥ **INVITATION:** Write these compassionate responses down and keep them somewhere visible. Remind yourself daily that meeting your grief with understanding is a nurturing, healing act. Return to these words when the emotion feels unimaginable.

July 16

If you're considering adopting another animal to "quit grieving," hoping that a new companion will "fix" your emotional pain, or you're feeling uncertain if you "deserve" a new companion, or you're fearing potential resentment, these are important signals to respect. Examining these feelings can guide your next steps in adopting.

♥ **INVITATION:** Journal about your emotional readiness. How are you coping with grief, and are you prepared for a new connection? Discern if it's truly "no" or grief that arises, as this insight will help you make the best decision.

July 17

Think about the narratives you've encountered regarding grief from others or those you've internalized. Consider which messages support you and which you wish to reject. For the ones you don't find beneficial, how would you rewrite them? Which align with and impact your grief the most?

♥ **INVITATION:** Pour your favorite grief messages and beliefs into a grief care manifesto using the voice of your most compassionate self. This could be a rant, haiku, list, or mantras—whatever feels right. Use this manifesto as a reminder that you are permitted to experience this grief on your terms.

July 18

Close your eyes and breathe deeply. Imagine your grief as a dense star, slowly expanding and glowing. Just as stars give birth to new light, your grief holds the potential for new beginnings, for tenderness, and for understanding that the love you share with your beloved maintains its radiance even in the darkest times.

♥ **INVITATION:** Write or speak about how your beloved's light continues to shine.

July 19

Never miss an opportunity to connect with your beloved through meaningful gestures. Personalized items, such as monogrammed keepsakes or engraved jewelry, can bring daily smiles. Consider creating customized memorabilia like wind chimes, photo blankets, or mugs to honor your beloved's memory. These small, personal touches can offer delight and solace during your grief.

♥ **INVITATION:** Choose something to personalize in honor of your beloved and introduce it to your space as a reassuring reminder.

July 20

What you do with your beloved's remains is entirely your choice. Whether you choose not to receive them, display them in an urn, scatter them in the ocean, bury them in your yard, incorporate them into artwork, or keep them out of sight, the decision is yours. Trust your choice. You owe no one an explanation. If you're feeling pressured, consider this your permission slip to do what feels right.

♥ **INVITATION:** How can you honor your beloved's remains in a way that feels true to your connection?

July 21

Identifying helpful thoughts is crucial because they're often drowned out by negative noise. These quiet yet powerful insights can ground you when waves of grief rock you. By intentionally seeking and embracing these supportive thoughts, you create a foundation of resilience that strengthens you.

♥ **INVITATION:** List your least and most supportive thoughts from recent days, then highlight those that truly uplift you. Nurture and reinforce these helpful thoughts to guide you through tough times by speaking three of them out loud each day.

July 22

Your beloved may have been your guide to new experiences and friendships, urging you to venture and embrace the beauty around you. With them by your side, you may have gained strength and inspiration to live a more connected, vibrant life, nurturing your soul and sense of belonging. Choose one way to honor their legacy by connecting outwardly today. Reach out to a friend, explore a new place, or engage with nature.

♥ **INVITATION:** Write three small things you plan on doing to deepen your relationship with the world.

July 23

Dreams and plans that will never come to fruition can leave an ache in your heart. Today, try completing one task, start to finish. Choose something tactile that engages your body—this can feel especially satisfying to your weary mind. Notice how it feels to complete something fully.

♥ **INVITATION:** Write a letter to your beloved about what feels unfinished between you two. Afterward, brainstorm ways to honor your relationship and those incomplete moments.

July 24

You deserve love, happiness, and self-care. You are valuable and worthy, and you have gifts to offer both yourself and the universe. You deserve to set boundaries, release what doesn't serve you, and embrace your imperfections. Celebrate yourself as you are and recognize that you are not alone. Your needs matter and you're not required to change for anyone.

♥ **INVITATION:** Add any additional reminders that speak to you to this list. Create your own version of this pep talk and place it somewhere you'll see it daily.

July 25

Astrology offers a gentle way to find meaning and connection. Exploring your beloved's sun sign, if known, or reviewing planetary events can help you to understand their essence. Events like full moons, retrogrades, or seasonal shifts each carry qualities that can offer comfort. Understanding your own sun sign and chart may also support grief, guiding you toward strengths and insights for healing.

♥ **INVITATION:** Research your beloved's sun sign or choose a planetary symbol for them. Consider these qualities alongside your own and journal about your discoveries.

July 26

"Progress" in grief is difficult to define, as it's not a linear path but rather a mix of uphill and downhill moments. Social media may tempt you to compare your highlights and lowlights to others, but remember, your road is uniquely yours. Remember the early days of your grief and notice the shifts that have occurred since. You're voyaging as you're meant to, so patience with yourself is key.

♥ **INVITATION:** Make a timeline of your grief experience, indicating both the highs and lows. What's it like to revisit each peak and valley?

July 27

Find a quiet space and set out three candles: one for you, one for your beloved, and one for your shared relationship. Take a few deep breaths. Light the candle for yourself, saying, *This flame is my light—my strength, my growth, my path forward.* Light the candle for your beloved, saying, *This flame is the light of your spirit—our bond, your memory, and the love we share.* Light the candle for your relationship, saying, *This flame is the light of our connection—eternal, transforming, and filled with love.*

❤ **INVITATION:** Once the candles burn down, use the melted wax to create a painting symbolizing this ritual and your connection.

July 28

Place your hand over your heart and feel your heartbeat. Tune in to this rhythm of life, allowing it to remind you of your strength and perseverance. Ask yourself aloud: *What does my heart need in this moment of grief?*

❤ **INVITATION:** Create a small box where you keep items or symbols or what your heart needs each day. Add a note, sacred item, or image each time you connect with your heart's needs, building a personal collection of reminders to honor your experience.

July 29

Grief can feel like opening a box of tangled necklaces, each chain leading to different aspects of your life. As you pull at one strand, it uncovers other losses—past cities, past relationships, past jobs, past transitions, or the person you once were. These links are all connected, melded together by your life. It can feel like many chapters are closing as you mourn. Recognize each chain of grief that is part of your current constellation.

♥ **INVITATION:** How might you honor each chain of grief?

July 30

Sometimes, we long for signs from our beloved and wonder why they feel distant. Though understandings of these communications remain unknown, remember that when we're struggling, it's often hard to feel the presence of those we love. In high states of stress or dysregulation, we focus on survival, which can block our awareness of gentle signs. By tending to yourself with kindness—resting, nourishing, and hydrating—you create space, opening the door for deeper moments of connection and presence.

♥ **INVITATION:** Close your eyes, take a few breaths, and ask yourself: *What can I do to make more space for receiving signs from my beloved?*

July 31

The love you have for your beloved is like water carving its way through a canyon—steady, powerful, and ever-deepening. It doesn't diminish with time or distance. Instead, it alters and strengthens, finding new paths as you honor your relationship. This love pours through you, guiding you through the toughest moments.

❤ **INVITATION:** Write a letter to your beloved, expressing how your love for them has grown and evolved since their transition. Share how they continue to influence your life and how you plan to carry your relationship into the world.

August 1

During grief, your mind can become a whirlwind of "what-ifs." While it's natural to question, it's also important to anchor yourself in the reality of the love and care you provided. Your beloved's earthside life was infinitely better because you were their guardian. Reinforcing this can help shift your focus from regret to appreciation and gratitude for your role and the time you shared together.

♥ **INVITATION:** Write down three positive impacts you had on your beloved's life. Appreciate these contributions and how they enriched your beloved's existence.

August 2

Let your anger take up space. Yell, cry, and break things. Scream underwater or punch pillows. Bash magazines with a baseball bat. Releasing stored-up wrath is important during grief. However, you want to liberate it; don't be gentle—let it rip! Be careful not to hurt yourself or others, of course.

♥ **INVITATION:** If you have a local rage room available, book a session! If you don't have one where you live, DIY with objects you can destroy in a safe space.

August 3

Hold an object that connects you to your beloved—perhaps a photo, collar, or another heirloom. Close your eyes and gently explore its texture, smell, and weight. Let the memories flow through you. Ask: *What message does this carry for me today?* Stay with whatever emotions arise, allowing the object to anchor you.

💜 **INVITATION:** After spending time with the saved item, write down any messages, memories, or feelings it stirs.

August 4

The next time you encounter a tree, take a moment to breathe with it. They need our carbon dioxide exhalations for their nourishment, just as we need the oxygen they release into the world. Take a moment to commune, calmly inhaling the gifts the tree offers you and slowly exhaling the nutrients you offer the tree. If it feels supportive, touch the trunk and say thank you as you connect.

💜 **INVITATION:** Imagine your beloved alongside you and invite them to tree-breathe with you.

August 5

You know your beloved's desires and indulgences. Channel that knowledge into a scavenger hunt in their honor. Include items like signature color objects, favorite treats, or stuffed animals, and consider adding symbolic items that represent their attitude or a lesson they taught you. A scavenger hunt can be especially meaningful on milestone days.

♥ **INVITATION:** Invite others to join in the fun to memorialize your beloved as a group. You can offer snazzy prizes that showcase your beloved's spirit to the winners.

August 6

Grief is like carrying a slippery boulder that requires constant adjustment, yet you find the stamina to keep moving. You've never carried it before and don't know how long the rock will remain so heavy. Each time you modify your grip, you reflect your resilience and deep love for your beloved. Commend yourself on how you're adjusting to carry your grief.

♥ **INVITATION:** Write down the "muscles" you've used—whether it's accepting help from others, finding solace in routines, or embracing quiet moments. Acknowledge your power and consider sharing your insights with someone who understands.

August 7

Getting to know ourselves after our beloved's transition can feel daunting, yet embracing different parts of who we are is an act of compassion. Do you notice your playful side, your wounded child, your intuitive nurturer, radiant creator, or your fierce advocate? Examining these aspects of yourself allows you to honor the full spectrum of emotions and experiences you hold, creating supportive space for your identity.

♥ **INVITATION:** Make a list of the parts of yourself you want to recognize. Begin each with *One part of me is* . . . and offer each one gratitude, promising to nurture and honor them as you progress.

August 8

Showing yourself compassion might feel as foreign as learning a new language. You may be accustomed to holding yourself to high standards, pushing for perfection, or feeling frustrated when you don't measure up. Benevolence, reassurance, and patience might seem out of place. But remember, these are the qualities your beloved showered upon you. They saw your worth and knew you deserved gentle understanding, and they weren't mistaken.

♥ **INVITATION:** What do you most need to hear today? Stand in front of your mirror and imagine your beloved beside you. Say aloud your most needed words. Repeat them for one minute and allow them to truly bolster you.

August 9

It's natural to feel closer to one animal over another, and it doesn't make you a bad guardian to have a "favorite." If your favorite transitioned, build your bond with your surviving companion and allow room for your bond to blossom. They are here and are an important link to your beloved. Celebrate their unique gifts and role in your life and remain open to new possibilities with them.

♥ **INVITATION:** What daily gratitude practice can you start with your surviving animal? Begin with: *Thank you, [Companion's Name], for being here. I love you and am grateful for your presence.*

August 10

What we control is often limited to what's "inside our hula hoop." We can't control people, their reactions, the past, the circumstances of our beloved's transition, or the future. But you can control your body, desires, responses, thoughts, beliefs, actions, and how you choose to celebrate, memorialize, and continue your relationship with your beloved.

♥ **INVITATION:** What's something you've been attempting to control that you can release today?

August 11

The fear of forgetting your beloved is common and can seem insurmountable. From the smell of their paws to the feel of their scratchy tongue, to your highlights and quiet moments—preserving it all feels urgent. Creating a tangible record of your memories can help.

♥ **INVITATION:** Grab a large piece of paper—big enough to cover a door frame. Tape it up and write down every memory you want to keep. When one sheet is full, cover another door and keep going. Let these memories be seen, as big as your love.

August 12

If you endured anticipatory grief before your beloved transitioned, you might still be grappling with its aftermath. Complex emotions like uncertainty, fear, hypervigilance, powerlessness, anger, and sorrow may have strained you. It's difficult to feel like you handled everything perfectly or stayed entirely attentive. Recognizing how hard that time was is not a betrayal to your beloved. Now, as you grieve, soothe this part of your experience with the gift of kindness and grace.

♥ **INVITATION:** Write a letter of self-compassion about how challenging your anticipatory grief was.

August 13

Limiting beliefs, such as "I shouldn't be so upset," "It's all my fault," or "No one will understand," can exacerbate your pain. To move through your grief, it's crucial to stop listening to these harmful messages and instead focus on self-compassion, kindness, and patience. If limiting beliefs arise, ask yourself: *What if this isn't right? How is this belief helping me? What belief can I adopt that's more loving and tender?*

♥ **INVITATION:** Reframe one limiting belief today into a self-compassionate thought.

August 14

When desolation strikes, close your eyes and imagine your beloved before you. Set a one-minute timer. Close your eyes and focus on anything you can hear around you. Visualize stroking your beloved, breathing with them. Then, focus your attention on your breath. Allow each exhalation to release loneliness and each inhale to fill you with love, awakening the energy of self-compassion, reminding yourself your breath is always with you. Between breaths, repeat the phrase, *I am here for you.* When the timer completes, thank yourself for taking care of you.

♥ **INVITATION:** Ask your beloved to stay near you for the day, offering their reassuring influence as they always have.

August 15

If you experience a tough day, week, or month, you might fear you're "backsliding." Grief involves fluctuating emotions and even on difficult days, you are still moving with it. When feeling stuck, remind yourself that grief isn't linear. Acknowledge that every step, forward or backward, is an important part of your experience.

❤ **INVITATION:** Find a peaceful nook and gently close your eyes. Envision a sanctuary that fills you with calm and joy—perhaps a cozy spot with your beloved. Immerse yourself in the sights, sounds, scents, and sensations of this place. Let your body relax and your breath slow, giving your mind a restful escape. When the scene is clear, softly affirm to yourself: *I am making progress. I am proud of myself.*

August 16

During grief, hearing and being counseled by your sage inner voice can be difficult. This voice isn't the critical part of you—it's your wise self, communicating from a place of silence and wisdom within. To hear it, you must quiet your mind and free it from worry, stress, and fear. Practice listening to this subtle voice; it often whispers and requires calm to be understood.

❤ **INVITATION:** Open your heart with love and gratitude, then listen. How has your inner voice supported you so far?

August 17

Sit quietly with the grief feelings wheel on page 221, eyes closed. Let your hand hover, placing a finger on an emotion without looking. Consider how this feeling connects to your grief. Is it familiar or new? Think of memories with your beloved linked to this feeling and any other strong memories from other chapters of your life.

♥ **INVITATION:** Write down your reflections about and relationship to this emotion and its impact on your grief. Revisit this exercise weekly to notice shifts in your emotional landscape.

August 18

Grief can heighten feelings of isolation. In these moments, remind yourself that the universe is here to support your sorrow, healing, and growth. It's ready to nourish, teach, and steady you when you're hurting. Even if you are unsure about your broader beliefs, discover if leaning in to the idea of the universe as a place that can hold and balm your sorrow feels supportive.

♥ **INVITATION:** Write, *I trust the universe to* . . . and regard how you can depend on its support more fully, letting it cradle you through this time.

August 19

Place one hand on your chest and the other on your abdomen. Breathe deeply and imagine holding your grief between your hands, acknowledging its presence without pushing it away. Ask yourself: *What do I need to feel more connected to my heart right now?* Notice any sensations or impressions that surface as you cradle your grief gently.

♥ **INVITATION:** : Create a small visual representation of this feeling—whether through a simple drawing, a found object from nature, or a personal item. Let this physical symbol remind you of what you need to care for your heart.

August 20

When you're grieving, it's often hard to appreciate what's right in front of you. The weight of loss can make it difficult to see the beauty still present in your life. But no matter how extreme the grief, there are still flowers in your garden—those small moments, people, or things that bring light and comfort. Recognizing these flowers doesn't diminish your grief; it honors the balance of life, reminding you that even in sorrow, there is beauty.

♥ **INVITATION:** List all the flowers in your garden right now that you appreciate, and how their blossoms bring you delight.

August 21

Grief integrates into your life like lichens merging with rocks—over time, it becomes part of your foundation, quietly altering your landscape. Just as lichens create rich soil that nurtures new growth, your grief can cultivate a deeper connection with your beloved. This bond evolves with you, reminding you of enduring love. Welcoming the notion of integrating grief, rather than outrunning it, can lift a weight, allowing for a more significant, lasting bond.

♥ **INVITATION:** How would your grief look or feel different if your intention was integration?

August 22

Creating visual representations of yourself before and after your beloved and before and after your grief, helps you externalize the profound emotional shifts within. It allows you to ponder your path with new clarity, highlighting the ways your love and loss have shaped you. This process gives you a safe space to explore how grief transforms your identity, while honoring both who you were and who you are becoming.

♥ **INVITATION:** Create a painting or drawing of yourself "before" and "after" your beloved, and then do the same for "before" and "after" your grief. Study the changes in each rendering and what they reveal.

August 23

Your beloved's "welcome home" salutation was as unique as a fingerprint, a special ritual that affirmed the adoration between you. Recalling these "hellos" can spark blissful reflection. What a gift to feel so acknowledged and appreciated! If it feels supportive, continue to greet your beloved using your favorite nicknames and exclamations.

❤ **INVITATION:** List your beloved's "greeting rituals." Describe the actions, sounds, and emotions involved. Revisit them whenever you need a boost.

August 24

Who informs your understanding and what are the origin stories for your prominent grief beliefs? It's a common misconception that all-consuming sadness best honors our beloved. Grief is multifaceted, incorporating both sadness and moments of joy. Just as your beloved brought happiness into your life, allow yourself to smile, laugh, and find lightness amidst anguish. Mourning and delight are interconnected, and both are allowed.

❤ **INVITATION:** When did you learn that amusement or glee couldn't co-exist with grief? Who taught that to you?

August 25

Struggling with decision-making is common. Practice building confidence by seeing decisions as doorways to growth rather than obstacles. Clarify your thoughts by exploring your options, and trust your intuition—you know what's right for you. Moving forward, take small steps and adjust as you go. Be gentle with yourself and tune in to what you genuinely want, allowing each choice to reflect your authenticity.

♥ **INVITATION:** Reflect on past decisions. How did you navigate them, and would you choose the same path again?

August 26

Pressing into the earth or a solid surface can help ground you. By pressing your feet into the floor in a deep yoga squat or your palms together in prayer, you stimulate your body's nervous system, bringing you back to the present. When feeling disconnected or angry, press your feet or hands firmly against a wall and feel the earth pressing back, offering support. This physical engagement pulls you out of emotional numbness and into your body, creating a sense of stability and safety.

♥ **INVITATION:** Try a pressing pose today and notice how it grounds you.

August 27

Consider universal truths that uplift you—like *I am never truly alone, Love knows no boundaries,* or *Each moment holds renewal.* These might come from spiritual traditions or your own inner knowing. Embrace the truths that bring you a sense of peace and let them walk alongside you as you mourn.

♥ **INVITATION:** Write down five universal truths that define you. Which ones help you feel held and championed? Lean into those when grief feels especially heavy.

August 28

As you notice your personal growth during grief, you might wonder, *Why did my beloved have to die for me to become "better?"* If this thought crosses your mind, remember: you are not evolving because your beloved died—you are evolving because they lived. Like a flower nourished by sunlight, your growth is fueled by the love and life you shared. There are countless ways you've grown because they lived and loved you.

♥ **INVITATION:** How do you notice the contributions from your beloved shaping you as you move with your grief?

August 29

Research shows that music engages areas of the brain tied to memory, mood, and emotional regulation. Listening to music can release dopamine, the "feel-good" chemical, which helps ease sadness and lift your spirits. Music also activates the parasympathetic nervous system, calming anxiety and creating a soothing effect. Whether it's to comfort, energize, or reflect, music can guide us back to emotional balance. Create a playlist based on the emotional state or mental space you want to cultivate today.

♥ **INVITATION:** Make a list of songs that help shift your mood, for example, from bitter to peaceful or anxious to serene.

August 30

If a movement practice, such as dancing, hiking, or biking supported you before your beloved's transition, invite your beloved to be included in a new way now, even if you're not feeling inspired. Movement practices release stress hormones and generate endorphins so it's supportive to keep engaging with them, even in grief's exhaustion.

♥ **INVITATION:** Next time you put your body in motion, engage your beloved, whether that's putting their collar on your yoga mat, sticking a photo of them on your bike, or listening to their playlist while you run.

August 31

A milestone—like an anniversary, birthday, or gotcha day—can stir powerful emotions, often increasing as the day approaches. When the day arrives, it may feel impossible to do anything—even to get out of bed—and that's okay. Be flexible and compassionate with yourself. If retreating or adjusting plans feels supportive, honor that need. Remember, celebrating your beloved on a different day is just as meaningful.

♥ **INVITATION:** Repeat this mantra: *I allow this milestone to unfold as it's meant to, and I can honor my beloved on another day if I need to.*

Grief often calls you to release what was to welcome what is yet to come. The act of releasing invites you to honor shifting energy and allow yourself to move with the flow of nature. Let go of things that deplete your energy to welcome things that will nurture it. Let go of any guilt, resentment, or negative feelings so you can welcome in healing, love, and opportunity.

Use this time to embody resilience and navigate with your beloved as your guiding light. Be kind to yourself and continue to deepen your connection with your beloved by doing things that enliven your relationship. Cultivate rituals that foster connection, such as walking on a familiar path or snuggling with one of their heirlooms while you journal. The act of releasing is not about forgetting your beloved or relinquishing their memories; it's about shedding the guilts and harmful thoughts that keep you feeling stuck in pain. It's about allowing yourself to honor your beloved with love and kindness.

Visualize the love you share filling your home as you welcome changes into your life and adjust to your beloved's transition. Be grateful for the lessons they taught you and continue to teach you. As you continue your grieving experience, consider how you can gather and venerate the gifts and lessons of your beloved.

September

September 1

Sit comfortably, close your eyes, and take a few deep breaths. Imagine a glimmering, golden cord extending from your heart, reaching out until it connects to your beloved's spirit. Visualize this thread glowing with vibrant energy—a soul-to-soul link, alive and eternal, holding the love that can never be broken. Feel their presence on the other end, a comforting warmth flowing back to you along this radiant connection. Let yourself rest in this bond, knowing that their love and light are with you always.

♥ **INVITATION:** When you feel alone, return to this golden cord. Imagine its warmth, and let it remind you of your beloved's presence, a connection that endures.

September 2

Grief can feel like navigating a dark cave where every step is uncertain. Who am I without my beloved? Will I ever feel whole again? Will the loneliness ever ease? Yet within you, strengths grow like stalactites and stalagmites, slowly forming solid pillars from above and below, bolstering you. The places where you feel incomplete are like the slow growth of these columns, gradually building into something enduring.

♥ **INVITATION:** Draw your cave. What stalactites and stalagmites are forming? What are the names of each pillar?

September 3

In grief, we often carry the voices and influences of those who shaped us—both positively and negatively. Reflecting on these influences can reveal how we view ourselves and the world during our heartache. Who are the five most influential people in your life, whether they offered affection or caused pain? How have they shaped your self-perception and your approach to grief? Understanding these influences helps you see where you may be holding on to ideas that no longer serve you.

♥ **INVITATION:** In your journal, reflect on how these five people have impacted your grief journey. What can you emancipate, and what can you honor?

September 4

Rest your hands over your heart, butterfly style, and gently tap four times on your right side, then four times on your left. Continue the alternating tapping, then ask yourself: *What would feel most supportive to me in this moment?* The answer might be obvious, or it might surprise you. If your inner critic questions or dismisses what feels supportive, release that judgment and trust your own wisdom.

♥ **INVITATION:** Make a list of supportive ideas. You don't need to act on them immediately, but it can become a powerful list to revisit when you're wondering how to sustain yourself in a challenging moment.

September 5

You can use the five love languages to continue your relationship with your beloved. Acts of service could involve volunteering in their honor; words of affirmation might be writing them letters; quality time could be spent in places they loved; physical touch could be snuggling their favorite blanket; and gifts might be creating a memorial. Experimenting with which love language resonates the most can be eye-opening for your honoring.

♥ **INVITATION:** Embrace your beloved's primary love language and create a ritual that honors it.

September 6

It's common to dwell on the "what ifs," wishing for more moments or different experiences with your beloved. Yet, every second you shared was steeped in love and connection. Grievers often yearn for more time, but the truth is, no amount of time would ever feel enough. Instead, treasure the days you had—they were precious and brimming with wonder.

♥ **INVITATION:** Calculate the number of earthside days you spent with your beloved. Celebrate this signature number, holding it close to your heart as a symbol of your enduring bond.

September 7

Boundaries are essential in grief, particularly for protecting your emotional well-being. Setting clear limits with others—whether about discussing your experience or needing time for yourself—helps create a safe space for you. Boundaries are an act of self-respect and self-care, honoring both your needs and your grief.

♥ **INVITATION:** Write down one or two boundaries to establish, and practice communicating them gently but firmly to those around you.

September 8

Imagine yourself as clay, molded by your beloved into who you are today. Without them, you would be fundamentally different. Their presence and love have shaped you, smoothing rough edges and deepening your form, granting new appreciations and capacities. Even in their absence, their impressions remain, solidifying your strength and resilience. Remembering this can offer solace on challenging days.

♥ **INVITATION:** Write a declaration to your beloved, starting each line with *Because I met you* . . . and describe all the ways they have reshaped your life.

September 9

Pinpointing where you are and where you want to be can be revealing. Feeling stuck, exhausted, or numb can make it difficult to imagine experiencing peace, reassurance, or joy. Approach yourself kindly and recognize that each small choice you make daily can guide you toward these new feelings. Your path from where you are now to where you wish to be is mapped by these compassionate steps.

♥ **INVITATION:** Using the grief feelings wheel on page 221, list the emotions you're currently experiencing and those you wish to feel. Identify one concrete action you can take to move toward each of the emotions you desire.

September 10

Visions, fantasies, and hopes seem to evaporate when your beloved transitions, especially if the loss is unexpected. Loose ends and unresolved feelings may emerge as envy, anger, or a sense of being cheated. It can be restorative to honor the loss of these future aspirations by acknowledging their power and significance.

♥ **INVITATION:** Write a list of the dreams you had with your beloved beginning with, *Here are some of the dreams I had* . . . and read it aloud. Then, write a second list starting with, *Here are some of the dreams I have* . . . and share it aloud too.

September 11

Picture a challenging time when your beloved stood by you, like a steady anchor in a storm, their presence grounding you in the midst of hardship. The fortitude they offered then is still with you, an unseen but deeply felt force that continues to steady you.

♥ **INVITATION:** Write about this challenging time and how your beloved supported you through it. Celebrate the power they gave you and consider how you can carry it forward, letting their love continue to anchor you in difficult moments.

September 12

If you were not able to say goodbye, remember that you expressed love, kindness, and adoration every single day you were with your beloved. Your words, from sweet nicknames to heartfelt declarations, and your care, whether it was through developing fun games or adventuring together, showed your beloved their importance. Each moment shared was a testament to your devotion, and when "goodbye" crosses your mind, remind your beloved "I love you," instead.

❤ **INVITATION:** Celebrate the loving exchanges you shared daily. Write them down as a reminder of the constant veneration felt between you.

September 13

Choose three animals to symbolize different aspects of yourself in grief: one for how you move, one for how you feel, and one for how you think. Meditate on the strengths of each animal and how they correlate to you. Consider how their strengths can assist your coping and imagine how your chosen animals might coexist in your emotional landscape.

❤ **INVITATION:** Sketch these creatures and their environments on paper—don't worry about making it look perfect or professional. The goal is expression, not perfection.

September 14

What would it look like to show up as your beloved in your daily life? Imagine roving through the world as they did—admiring what enchanted them, offering amusement to everyone you encounter. How extraordinary to show up in the world with the same grace and generosity they offered.

♥ **INVITATION:** Intentionally embody your beloved's essence today in some part of your life. What does it feel like to be them?

September 15

Animal loss is often considered "disenfranchised" grief, meaning it's not widely acknowledged or supported by society. This can leave you feeling isolated, minimized, or even ashamed. It's common to not receive sympathy cards, food offerings, or bereavement leave, adding to the loneliness.

♥ **INVITATION:** Generate a list of all the cultural, public, and social support you believe every grieving guardian deserves. What do you wish for anyone going through this? What do you wish you had at this moment?

September 16

Integrating your inner child into daily life promotes self-compassion and eases self-criticism. Seeing a photo of your younger face serves as a gentle reminder to offer yourself the same tenderness you would to that child. Embrace the innocence, vulnerability, and courage that still live within you.

♥ **INVITATION:** Place a photo of your younger self somewhere visible, such as your bathroom mirror or phone lock screen. How would you care for that child and extend that same kindness, warmth, and understanding to yourself today?

September 17

Choose a daily task and turn it into a ritual that honors your beloved. Use cleaning supplies in their signature color, place a photo pillow on the bed when you make it, or brush your teeth with a photo of them in your medicine cabinet. These gestures transform everyday tasks into moments of connection, keeping your beloved's spirit vibrant in your daily life.

♥ **INVITATION:** Choose one daily "chore" to transform and observe how it brings stability and energy to your relationship with your beloved.

September 18

Grief can be challenging for others to understand, often due to society's discomfort with discussing death and loss. This leaves many unsure of how to support someone grieving, sometimes causing them to avoid or minimize your pain. Some fear saying the "wrong" thing, while others may feel uneasy with their own past losses. When someone doesn't acknowledge your beloved, it often reflects their discomfort, not your grief's value.

♥ **INVITATION:** Gently consider sharing your needs with those you trust—whether hearing your beloved's name, listening to a cherished memory, or simply being present. These small acts help others honor your journey authentically.

September 19

It's easy to fill our time with distractions that don't truly support our grief. We may find ourselves slipping into routines that keep us busy but don't help us mourn. To care for our hearts, we must gently examine how we're spending our time and ask: *Do these activities nurture my grief?* Being intentional with our time allows us to make space for healing, even in the smallest moments.

♥ **INVITATION:** : Reflect on one daily habit that may distract you from grieving. How can you transform it into something more helpful?

September 20

If your beloved has special heirlooms they cherished—whether bow ties, catnip bananas, spring toys, or plushies—consider displaying their treasures prominently in your home or workspace. Showcasing these items serves as a constant reminder of your beloved's delight and the consideration with which you selected them.

❤ **INVITATION:** Select a shadowbox or display case for your beloved's favorite keepsakes. Arrange these sacred heirlooms where you can appreciate them daily, commemorating their significance in your life.

September 21

Deciding to welcome a new animal while grieving is complex. While none can replace your beloved, each offers unique gifts and lessons. If you believe your beloved arrived in your life at the right moment, perhaps the same will be true for your next companion. Trusting that the right companion will come at the right time can be challenging. Reflecting on your beloved's arrival might offer reassurance.

❤ **INVITATION:** Write a letter to your future family member, welcoming them when you are both ready. Share your vision for this new relationship and consider sharing the letter with your beloved for their insights.

September 22

Just as an oyster transforms an irritant into a pearl, your grief can reshape the pain of your beloved's transition into something meaningful. Each layer of love, memory, and connection you foster becomes part of a precious tribute to your bond. Over time, anguish softens, crafting pearls of wisdom, strength, and enduring devotion in your heart.

❤ **INVITATION:** As your grief develops, can you see any tiny pearls forming in your heart? What are their names?

September 23

Recollect how your beloved nurtured your emotions like a cozy blanket, enfolding you when you were inconsolable. Their quiet, intuitive understanding was always there, offering peace without words. In those moments, they knew exactly what you needed. This deep understanding you share still provides solace today.

❤ **INVITATION:** Create artwork that captures the warmth and comfort your beloved brought to your life. Use colors, textures, and images that remind you of their presence. Let each addition represent a moment when their presence wrapped around you like a cozy blanket.

September 24

Find a comfortable position and close your eyes. Take a deep breath, allowing your body to relax. Now, recall a recent moment of joy. Notice if any guilt arises alongside that joy. Acknowledge it without judgment. Imagine your beloved with you. What would they say about your happiness? Hear their voice reminding you that bliss doesn't diminish your love or connection.

♥ **INVITATION:** Each time guilt emerges, pause and ask your beloved how they would want you to feel. Let their love guide you in releasing guilt and embracing delight.

September 25

It's instinctive to wonder how to find meaning without your beloved's earthside presence. This moment is a possibility to rewrite old scripts that are not helpful to you. Just as a wind prunes dead branches to make way for new growth, you can make supportive choices in your grief. For example, if you declare: *No one will ever love me as much as my beloved did,* try reframing it as, *Our love was unique, and love is infinite. I will love and be loved again.*

♥ **INVITATION:** Identify a belief that might be holding you back. How can you reframe it to support your healing?

September 26

Every place and journey you shared, like pieces of a collage, added new fragments to your larger story. Every adventure contributed a unique tone and contour to the mosaic of your relationship with each location capturing a moment in time. Chart these expeditions on a physical or digital map or in a custom book, distinguishing significant spots with notes or pictures. Let this cartography become a visual mosaic, celebrating the distinctive and colorful story you created together.

♥ **INVITATION:** Frame a photo with engraved coordinates, display a custom star map, or create a memory jar filled with sand or soil from a sacred location.

September 27

Is there something small you can look forward to today? Maybe it's a new album, a visit from a friend, or an upcoming trip. These moments of anticipation are like rays of sunshine breaking through clouds, offering relief from the heaviness of grief. Where can you find a brief respite of gladness?

♥ **INVITATION:** If you're struggling to find something to anticipate, ask yourself: *What brings me pleasure, makes me happy, calms me, or makes me laugh?* These answers could lead you to new, promising pathways for ease.

September 28

Dreams can be powerful messengers during grief, offering insight, connection, and emotional processing when our waking mind feels swamped. Recording your dreams helps you tune in to emotions or thoughts you may not consciously recognize and may even bring moments of comfort or connection with your beloved. Grief often revamps our dream life, allowing a deeper exploration of our inner world and the emotions we might be holding.

♥ **INVITATION:** Keep a dream journal by your bedside. Each morning, write down anything you remember—images, feelings, or details—and notice what patterns or messages emerge.

September 29

Close your eyes and gently scan your body from head to toe. Notice the sensations—tightness, heaviness, or warmth. Is your heart racing, or are your shoulders tense? Grief often speaks through the body before we name the emotions. Take a slow, deliberate breath, letting it calm your mind. Inhale for four, hold for seven, and exhale for eight. As your body relaxes, ask yourself: *How am I feeling right now?* without judgment. Then, try naming your emotions, using the grief feelings wheel on page 221 if needed.

♥ **INVITATION:** Notice patterns between your body's sensations and your grief. How can you assist what you're feeling today?

September 30

Children's grief often comes in waves, with emotions surfacing unpredictably. This rhythm is a natural part of their expression. By creating a supportive space that respects these shifts, you help them process feelings at their own pace. Follow their lead as they move between grief and other topics, providing a steady, accepting presence. Allowing them to choose how they say goodbye or honor their beloved gives them a sense of control. Activities like writing a note, drawing, or tending an altar honor their choices and strengthen their sense of agency.

♥ **INVITATION:** Engage your child in memorial projects, like scrapbooking or painting rocks.

167

SEPTEMBER

October 1

The first day of each month can feel crushing. There are milestones that will be missed, and it's one more month our beloved won't be physically alongside us. It reminds us of time passing and sometimes feeling farther away from our beloved than ever. Be extra generous with yourself today. You are not alone.

♥ **INVITATION:** Invest in additional self-care on the first day of this month. Plan a hike, massage, or a coffee date with friends.

October 2

Just as alchemists once sought to transform base metals into gold, early grief can feel like a volatile reaction, obscuring a future where your bond with your beloved flourishes. Even in this flurry of emotion, the potential for change remains. Imagine how your relationship might evolve, finding new ways to collaborate with your beloved as you navigate this alchemical process. Take solace in these possibilities, even if they seem uncertain.

♥ **INVITATION:** Write a letter of hope to your beloved, starting each sentence with *Someday* . . . and explore what could be possible for both of you in your advancing relationship.

October 3

Create a tranquil grief sanctuary for yourself—a portable space for when grief feels staggering. In those moments, it can be hard to know what we need, so having a ready-to-use sanctuary can provide support. Fill it with comforting items: a favorite poem, a snack, a soothing texture like a stress ball, or a crystal. Include suggestions like "Try box breathing," "Draw a tarot card," or "Stretch." You might also add notes like "You are enough" or "Rest tonight."

♥ **INVITATION:** Choose a vessel and begin creating your own mobile sanctuary today.

October 4

Acknowledging the experience of your beloved's final earthside moments can deepen your ongoing connection. That day was deeply significant and in the swirl of shock, sadness, and fear, you may feel there were things left unsaid or undone. If you find yourself judging your actions from those final days, invite self-compassion into your heart. Caregiving can leave us paralyzed by fear and hypervigilance, reacting instinctively in ways beyond our control. Remember, self-doubt often arises with hindsight—you couldn't have known then what you know now.

♥ **INVITATION:** Write two letters—one to your beloved and one from their perspective—acknowledging this day, honoring both difficulties and shared love. Read them aloud to give your experience witness.

October 5

What can you discover about your beloved's name? Whether you chose their name or they arrived with it, understanding new dimensions about their moniker can lead you to fresh insights and a deeper connection to their spirit and identity. It may even illuminate new signs and symbols to anticipate!

♥ **INVITATION:** Research your beloved's name across different cultures and languages. Explore its meaning, symbolism, and how it's used around the world. As you discover these variations, reflect on how they connect to your beloved's spirit or personality.

October 6

Ho'oponopono is an ancient Hawaiian practice of forgiveness and reconciliation, which can be healing. It involves repeating four phrases: *I'm sorry, Please forgive me, Thank you,* and *I love you.* This practice helps clear guilt, allowing you to focus on the love you share with your beloved.

♥ **INVITATION:** Try repeating these phrases daily, especially when guilt or regret arises, and notice how they help you relinquish and connect.

October 7

Maintaining your privacy during grief is essential. It's okay to keep things confidential until you're ready to share. Remember, you don't owe anyone details about your beloved's transition unless it feels supportive for your healing. Setting boundaries around sharing may feel hard but ultimately honors your experience and authenticity.

♥ **INVITATION:** Decide which aspects of your grief you wish to keep private. Memorize a supportive phrase for when others inquire, such as, "I appreciate your concern. It's difficult to discuss now; I'll share when or if I'm ready. Thanks for understanding."

October 8

Do you ever sense your beloved? Or get a tingle and wonder . . . is that a sign? If so, stay open! If not, stay open! Signs can cause tension, frustration, and comparison, especially in early grief. Not everyone experiences them when or how they want. Sometimes they're hard to recognize and it can take years for one to appear. If it's important to receive a sign, ask for one! And then, remain open to more.

♥ **INVITATION:** If you receive a sign, say, *More, please* or *Thank you, come again!* so your beloved knows to return.

October 9

Facing criticism can feel like defending a sandcastle from the tide. Criticism can sting, especially regarding your grief choices, expressions, and timeline. Remember, true support nurtures, not diminishes. If unwelcome comments arise, remind yourself that their words don't define your journey. Seek advice from those you trust, not from those who don't understand your heart.

♥ **INVITATION:** Identify who truly supports you and lean into their kindness when you need it most.

October 10

Grief can bring conflicting emotions, a concept known as "both/and thinking." You might feel relief and shock, anger and gratitude, guilt, and pride—all at once. These dualities are quintessential in grief. You are not being disloyal to your beloved if you have a wide range of emotional perceptions. You are fully experiencing the many textures of your relationship during grief. Welcoming them can help you navigate the complex wilderness you're traversing.

♥ **INVITATION:** Make a list that begins, *I am allowed to feel both* _____ *and* _____. Revere the many dualities you're balancing.

October 11

Engaging in hands-on activities like crafting, cooking, or creating art activates a large part of the brain's cortex, triggering the effort-driven reward circuit. This neurological system reinforces healthy behaviors and boosts psychological well-being. The more we engage in these physical tasks, the more our brains produce calming, satisfying effects. These activities can transform emotions into tangible expressions of our grief and our link to our beloved.

♥ **INVITATION:** Choose a creative activity, such as painting, knitting, or gardening, and dedicate it to your beloved. Share your creation with someone who will appreciate it.

October 12

Recall the comforting echoes of your beloved's presence—the jingle of their collar, the murmurs of their sleep, the thud of their paws on the counter, or the gentle lapping at their bowl. These familiar noises form a soothing symphony, whispering, "I am here."

♥ **INVITATION:** What can you do to re-create these sonic moments? It might warm your heart to pat the bed where a tail once swished or crinkle paper like a favorite toy. Become your own soundstage, bringing their soundtrack back to life, and see where it leads you.

October 13

Our beloveds encourage us to live in the moment, unburdened by past regrets or future worries. Their ability to be fully there with us enriches our lives and deepens our love. Inhabiting this mindset during grief is essential so that our mind doesn't wander to ruminating or future-tripping, as it naturally tends to do. If you can sustain the "right here, right now" mindset of your beloved, your grief may feel a bit lighter.

♥ **INVITATION:** What's one thing you can do today to live in the present?

October 14

Self-criticism can ignite when you're angry or envious around animals who remind you of your beloved. It's common to feel frustrated when others still have their companions while you don't. If you feel upset, jealous, or irritated, know that these sentiments are valid and part of your grieving process. Let these emotions flow without judgment, welcoming them as an essential aspect of your healing.

♥ **INVITATION:** Pour your feelings onto the page with a list that begins with, *I am jealous because* . . . or *I am annoyed because* . . . Let your emotions be attended and beheld.

October 15

Think about the seasonal activities you cherished together, like walks through nature, cozy nights in, or outdoor adventures. As you reminisce about these shared traditions, consider what seasonal ritual you might like to welcome right now, inviting their spirit to remain part of each.

♥ **INVITATION:** Create a living tribute by planting in their favorite color, whether it's with bulbs, seeds, or evergreen plants. As each time of year unfolds, you'll be greeted by vibrant symbols of your beloved's presence, bringing their spirit to life in your surroundings year-round.

October 16

What if you could be as authentic in your grief as you were with your beloved? Just as a waterfall cascades freely over rocks, let your grief flow naturally, without trying to contain or redirect it. Your beloved was genuine with you; now, allow yourself to be equally open in your sorrow. You don't need to dam your grief—let it pour out, knowing that every feeling is necessary.

♥ **INVITATION:** Journal about what it would be like to let your grief flow freely like a waterfall. How would it feel to disengage the need to control or hide it?

October 17

The tears you shed while you grieve your beloved are supporters. The release of tears activates your nervous system to help you regulate. Plus, tears activate oxytocin and endorphins to soothe and improve your mood. When you cry, you're tending to your grief and gifting yourself strength. There is no such thing as crying "too much." Your tears are a testament to your profound bond and ongoing relationship with your soulmate.

♥ **INVITATION:** Say this to yourself quietly or aloud: *Thank you, tears, for soothing me and providing release.*

October 18

Take a deep breath in through your nose and out through your mouth. As you breathe in, feel your lungs expand, and as you breathe out, let go of any tension. With each inhale, feel your body fill with life and energy. With each exhalation, release stress and anxiety. As you breathe in, remember your beloved's face, their favorite moments, and the wisdom they shared. As you breathe out, let go of sorrow and regret. Breathe in gratitude for them and breathe out gratitude for yourself.

♥ **INVITATION:** Repeat this exercise whenever you need a soothing break.

October 19

When someone makes a hurtful remark, assess their overall behavior and patterns in your life. Has this person generally been supportive or is this lack of consideration a pattern for them? Understanding this context can help you decide whether to address the issue immediately, wait to discuss it when your grief is less acute, or reconsider the relationship altogether. Consistency in behavior helps determine who is eligible to be a support to you.

♥ **INVITATION:** Assess your relationships and assess if any need re-evaluation based on their overall ability to show up and be a safe space for you.

October 20

Surveying your grief path is like peering through a prism, uncovering powerful realizations. Consider who you were on the day of your beloved's transition—your emotions, thoughts, and identity. As grief refracted through you, some parts may feel shattered, like light broken into pieces. Yet, just as a prism disperses light into a spectrum, your grief reveals facets of yourself you never noticed before.

♥ **INVITATION:** Write about who you were then that feels completely evolved. What aspects of your past self would you like to carry into your future? How has this prism of grief reshaped your identity?

October 21

Celebrate your beloved's protective instincts, like a vigilant guardian standing by you in times of uncertainty or dread. Their unwavering watchfulness was a shield of love—a testament to their deep dedication and care.

♥ **INVITATION:** Create an artwork that captures your beloved as your guardian, protector, or symbol of strength. Display this piece where it can offer you reassurance during moments of doubt—a reminder of their fierce love and the protection they still provide.

October 22

Fear can overpower in grief: the unknown, the dread of enduring such pain, and the worry that something similar could happen again. Just as your beloved explored life with inquisitive abandon, what would it be like to meet your fear with curiosity?

♥ **INVITATION:** When alarm arises, connect with a sacred object, like a crystal or a beloved's heirloom to ground yourself. If you feel brave, ask your fear: *What are you here to teach me?* See what message or feeling emerges.

October 23

Close your eyes and envision yourself one year from now, still carrying your beloved's memory, but having found relief from the early, acute layers of grief. Imagine the wisdom your future self holds. Ask: *What guidance do you have for me as I navigate this grief?* Allow yourself to feel held by your future self's compassion and understanding.

♥ **INVITATION:** Choose a small item—a stone or special token—that represents your future self. Carry it with you as a reminder of the guidance and growth you are imagining.

October 24

What messages are you receiving from society or culture about your experience? What are you subconsciously or directly hearing that impacts your grief? We absorb a lot of messaging when others learn we're grieving, and it can be powerful to extricate them by writing it all down. Take some time today to list the messages you've received during your grief.

♥ **INVITATION:** Review these messages and decide which ones to keep and which to release. How do they align with your own beliefs about grief?

October 25

Maintaining routine is crucial for surviving animals. Even as you struggle, keep their daily habits consistent. This period can also be an opportunity to introduce new activities that bring joy and distraction. New routines, like special training sessions, engaging toys, or enriching one-on-one time, can foster new bonds and offer comfort to both you and your companion.

♥ **INVITATION:** What new activity could you introduce to your surviving companion to enhance their routine and strengthen your rapport?

October 26

When anxiety arises, it's like a ripple in a still pond—your instinct might be to smooth it out or avoid the disturbance. But what if you allow the ripple to move across the surface, letting it settle naturally? By observing anxiety without trying to alter or suppress it, you can begin to understand its presence and what it might reveal.

♥ **INVITATION:** When you feel anxious, try sitting with it. Say: *I welcome my anxiety in. My anxiety has something to offer me.* Let it exist without judgment and be present with it.

October 27

El Día de los Muertos is a sacred holiday in Mexican and other Latin cultures for celebrating, honoring, and remembering loved ones. This holiday spans November 1 and November 2, but October 27 is the day believed to welcome the souls of animal companions back home. Building an ofrenda (a decorated altar) is a meaningful way to guide your beloved's spirit, using photos, candles, marigolds, and offerings that honor their memory. It's said these elements help your beloved find their way back to you for a loving visit.

♥ **INVITATION:** Research more about the elements of an ofrenda and create one with intention, including your beloved's favorite toys, signature colors, and cherished items. As you build it, visualize your beloved finding comfort and warmth in this special space.

October 28

It's natural to wonder what our beloved animals felt, but remember, their emotional experiences are different from ours. We often assume they respond as we would, projecting human reactions onto them. While there are similarities, animals express and process emotions uniquely. As we grieve, it's important to honor these differences, letting go of any human emotions we may have placed onto their experiences, freeing ourselves from unnecessary blame.

♥ **INVITATION:** Sit with an image of your beloved. Take deep breaths, focusing on your shared love. Visualize letting go of projected feelings, honoring their memory fully.

October 29

Reflect on blissful emotions, such as love, peace, or contentment. Using the grief feelings wheel on page 221, choose words that remind you of how you feel your beloved experienced life. Connect each jubilant word to a memory you shared together.

♥ **INVITATION:** Create a memory collage or journal entry for each feeling. Place it somewhere visible to remind you of the happiness your beloved brought and continues to bring to your life.

October 30

When faced with unanswered questions about your beloved's life, transition, or afterlife, choosing beliefs that bring solace can offer a sense of peace. Embracing "I choose to believe" allows you to find solace in beliefs that soothe rather than distress. Deciding on a perspective that feels right for you can help relieve the burden of uncertainty.

♥ **INVITATION:** List the beliefs you choose about your beloved, such as *I choose to believe we'll reunite someday* or *I choose to believe my beloved felt peace.* Remind yourself of how these choices support your serenity when challenging topics arise.

October 31

If you feel uneasy about attending a gathering or holiday event, share your concerns with those who care about you. Voicing your feelings may help ease some of the dread. You're allowed to handle events in any way that feels supportive to you.

♥ **INVITATION:** Customize and have this text ready to send before any upcoming occasion: *This is my first holiday/event without my beloved. I may need to take breaks or leave early. Please talk about [Companion's Name]; I love to hear their name and be reminded of memories. If I cry, remember my tears support me. You can hug me, squeeze my hand, or say something nice about my beloved. Thanks for understanding and caring about me.*

November 1

As you welcome in November, it might feel as if your beloved's memory could wither. Yet, each month ushers its own memories, milestones, and moments shared, renewing their presence in your life. Let this new month remind you that love remains, evolves with time, and is always part of your world.

♥ **INVITATION:** What activities, smells, and sights remind you of your beloved in November? Write these down to keep their spirit alive.

November 2

If corresponding with your beloved brings you closer, why not spice up your conversations with a fun, invigorating twist? There are many ways to chat with your beloved and letters are just the beginning.

♥ **INVITATION:** Consider writing an advice column about life events penned by your beloved, creating a dialogue conversation between you two, creating an adventurous story, making an ABC list of words that remind you of your beloved, writing music or movie reviews featuring your beloved's signature wit, or writing poems of all forms, including haikus, acrostics, or pantoums.

November 3

Activating your body in a new way during grief can support presence, reduce stress, and help release stagnant emotions. Physical movement promotes a sense of flow, allowing grief to process naturally rather than becoming stuck. Experiment with what feels best—whether high-energy or gentle movement—and notice how your emotions may shift as your body finds new outlets.

♥ **INVITATION:** Make a list of physical activities you'd like to try. From roller skating to rock climbing, hula dance to boxing, tai chi to tennis, find ways to move your body and open space for grief to transform.

November 4

You may have anger directed at someone specific: a family member, a care provider, or even your beloved. It's okay to be angry and it is not a betrayal of your relationships. Consider writing a "how dare you letter" that lets the recipient know just how angry you are. This is a letter you won't send or share.

♥ **INVITATION:** It might feel powerful to release this letter in a ritual, such as putting the message in a bottle or shredding it.

November 5

Your relationship with your beloved was predicated on laughter and humor. Allow this piece of your relationship to continue meaningfully as a way to stay connected and receive bliss.

♥ **INVITATION:** Designate a jar in your home to be your beloved's Giggle Jar. Anytime you think of something earthside they did that made you laugh, see something now that would delight them, or receive a silly sign, drop these laugh-inducing items into the jar. When the time is right, enjoy reading them aloud.

November 6

If you are experiencing multiple losses in a short amount of time through work as a foster, in a rescue, or in an animal care environment, the impact of repeated grieving can overwhelm. Give yourself the gift of creating small, meaningful rituals for each transition you experience.

♥ **INVITATION:** Choose a ritual for your next loss. You can try whispering a special blessing, anointing with sacred water or oils, crafting a photo tribute bulletin board, assembling a rock garden with a small stone painted for each transition, or hosting a yearly memorial service.

November 7

Your life has changed and you weren't given the chance to set the rules. Imagine grief as a waterslide—you can't change the slope, but you can adjust how you navigate the twists and turns. By being mindful of how you hold on, you can make the ride a bit smoother.

♥ **INVITATION:** List what you'd like to be different about your grief. Identify what's within your capability to shift, and start making changes. Empower yourself by improving one area today.

November 8

Never miss a chance to see your beloved's name in lights! Many companies and non-profits offer ways to make a permanent tribute. Paving stones, plaques, benches, theatre seats, or gardens can feature your beloved's name. You might also sponsor a habitat or adoptions at your local rescue or shelter—some may even let you include a photo.

♥ **INVITATION:** Call local organizations you admire and explore naming opportunities in your beloved's honor—or create your own idea and see if they're open to it.

November 9

What did your beloved enjoy most when they were earthside? Was it a favorite treat, a special place, or a beloved toy? Gather these memories and consider how you can incorporate them into your holiday traditions this year. Perhaps it's a dish at dinner in their honor or a sacred object in your tablescape. Your task is to bring their essence into your celebrations, keeping their story alive in every room.

♥ **INVITATION:** Make a list of your beloved's favorite things and find a way to highlight them in your holiday traditions. How will you honor them this season?

November 10

What does your relationship with yourself need to become more fulfilling? Loneliness might be weighing on you, but one way to ease that is by valuing your own company. You are worth spending time with. Even in the emptiness you feel, remember that when you're with yourself, you're with the person your beloved most cherished.

♥ **INVITATION:** What are three things you could do to become a nurturing friend to yourself?

November 11

Prayer objects like malas, rosaries, and worry beads have been used for centuries to deepen spiritual connection. Mala beads, from ancient India, guide meditation. The rosary, rooted in Christianity, aids contemplation. Greek worry beads provide a calming, tactile rhythm that eases the mind. These objects focus intentions and bring comfort. Holding your beloved's toy, collar, or a cherished item while connecting can also ground your feelings.

♥ **INVITATION:** Research sacred objects and choose or create one that feels right for you. As you connect, repeat: *May I find peace. May I feel love. May I honor the bond we share.*

November 12

If you are afraid good times will never come again, what do you imagine it would take to believe the opposite? You are capable of feeling good things; you deserve good things; and you have a tremendous capacity for happiness. You choose where your thoughts go. Endeavor to give yourself the support of thinking positive, hopeful thoughts, balancing any negative thoughts.

♥ **INVITATION:** When an upsetting thought arises, ask your beloved to release it for you and facilitate finding an encouraging replacement.

November 13

The search for fairness often leads to deeper suffering. Facing the "Why?" or "Why now?" confronts the randomness and seeming cruelty of transitioning. But what if you delicately shift to "Why *not* my beloved?" This isn't about dismissing your pain but acknowledging that loss is part of living. Embracing this may help you honor your bond and find peace in the impermanence of life cycles.

♥ **INVITATION:** What are you learning about your own beliefs relating to fairness and grief?

November 14

A powerful positive psychology exercise to boost resilience and supportive thinking is acknowledging what went well for you today and why, what it meant to you, or how to create more of it in the future. Journal this in the evening before saying goodnight to your beloved to help you unwind and feel thankful.

♥ **INVITATION:** Try writing a nightly "what went well and why" practice for one week.

November 15

Your critical voice may convince you there's only one outcome from a choice you did (or didn't) make. One decision could have changed everything; a different doctor would have had a different outcome; or one factor could have reversed the end. Often, there are multiple possibilities, and it can be helpful to be realistic about all the factors at play in your beloved's transition.

♥ **INVITATION:** If feelings arise about something you're "sure" of, write a list of alternative possibilities, options, and potential outcomes. If it feels good, assign likelihood percentages to each.

November 16

When you imagine the future for yourself and your grief, what do you envision? What grief "wins" or "turning points" do you aspire to? What will your relationship with your beloved look like as it unfolds and amplifies? How do you hope your grief will have changed as you've experienced it? Sometimes envisioning where we'd like to grow can be encouraging as we continue to move with our grief.

♥ **INVITATION:** Write a letter to your "future grief self" declaring where you hope to be. What comes up that you might be able to start enacting today?

November 17

Accepting your imperfections is an act of self-love. Recognize that you're human, with strengths and weaknesses, and that both are allowed. By accepting yourself as you are with kindness and understanding, you unshackle yourself from the pressure to be flawless and grant room for growth and authenticity.

♥ **INVITATION:** What are the parts of yourself you find difficult to accept? Why was it so easy for your beloved to accept them? Write about your relationship to these perceived imperfections and how they might actually contribute to your uniqueness.

November 18

Did your beloved offer you the nurturing you missed growing up? Perhaps they provided unconditional love, acceptance of your flaws, and reassurance in difficult times. They offered calm comfort, a consistent presence, and encouraged you to rest and play rather than please and perform. The hardest part of their transition may be feeling like these gifts will vanish, but they remain within you. Carry their legacy by loving yourself and others as they loved you.

♥ **INVITATION:** Write a letter to your beloved thanking them for all the ways they reparented you.

November 19

If your social activities revolved around your beloved, you might now feel a sense of purposelessness. Imagining purpose beyond your grief can be difficult, but being the keeper of your beloved's adventures and milestones can offer meaning. Keeping their joyful moments at the forefront may provide purpose as new parts of your identity assemble.

♥ **INVITATION:** Revisit a photo of a happy day with your beloved. Close your eyes and immerse yourself in the memory—what do you see, hear, smell, and feel? Stay in that moment, enjoying your beloved in this bliss. Remind yourself you can return anytime.

November 20

When you feel a gut-punch of aching, remind yourself, *This hurts, and it's okay to hurt.* If someone you loved were grieving, how would you support them? Can you offer this same kindness to yourself? And if you catch yourself engaging negatively, reroute and remind yourself to speak to yourself like a friend. Affirm your relationship with your beloved as you remind yourself: *I'm doing the best I can, and my best is enough.*

♥ **INVITATION:** Do something loving for yourself today.

November 21

Remember the first day you met your beloved—their eyes meeting yours, the first ethereal touch. This moment was the seed that grew into the deep connection you still carry today, a bond that continues as it always has, inviting growth and bliss with each new phase.

♥ **INVITATION:** Frame a photo from those early days and place it where you'll see it daily. Let this image be a touchstone, reminding you of the beautiful odyssey you began together and how it still shapes your life.

November 22

Bandwidth check: Are you ready for another animal? Welcoming a companion requires tremendous energy to help them adjust to being part of your family. Behavioral training, medical support, and adjustments to your routine, schedule, and lifestyle might feel like unwelcome surprises. It can also be exhausting to develop a bond with a new animal, especially if the connection isn't instant. If you're already low on capacity due to your grief, these types of shifts can be daunting and depleting.

♥ **INVITATION:** Brainstorm how it would look if your new companion were a complete 180 from your beloved in schedule, personality, challenges, abilities, and connection. What obstacles appear for your bandwidth when you consider this list?

November 23

Find a comfortable position and close your eyes. Focus on your breath, feeling the rise and fall of your chest. Now, imagine your beloved beside you, their essence warm and comforting. As you breathe in, feel their healing breath merging with yours; a gift of deep, reassuring energy. On each inhale, receive their breath—gentle, supportive, and filled with love. On each exhalation, release any tension, knowing they are here with you. Let their breath become a part of your own rhythm, a reminder of your connection and their unwavering presence.

♥ **INVITATION:** Repeat the mantra: *With each breath, I receive your love; with each breath, I feel your presence.* Let this mantra be a touchstone you can return to whenever you want to feel that divine energy again.

· · · · · · ·

November 24

Connection rituals with our beloveds are guides, not rules set in stone. As we grow and change, so too can our practices. Traditions that once brought comfort may no longer serve, and that's okay. Trust your intuition—skip, adapt, or create new ways of honoring your connection with your beloved. You are not obligated to stay the same—freedom within your grief is your right.

♥ **INVITATION:** Choose one connection ritual today and modify it. Try a new approach that feels aligned with your current emotions and needs. Notice how it feels to make this shift.

November 25

Lovely gestures and unexpected connections can be a surprising buoy in the sea of grief. Sometimes, meaningful support comes from the least likely places—through co-workers, relatives, or online communities. Have you been touched by someone's kindness after your beloved's transition? Showing gratitude to those who've made a difference can be a heartfelt way to honor them. It's a simple way to sprinkle more love into the world in your beloved's name.

♥ **INVITATION:** Who would you like to thank for supporting you in your grief?

November 26

Discover hidden connections in your beloved's name by rearranging the letters to unearth sweet surprises and treasures. It's a playful way to feel their presence on a new level, as anagrams can reflect their personality or inside jokes. Think of it as a celebration—a way to play with the letters they will always represent!

♥ **INVITATION:** Use a free generator to review the anagrams disguised in your beloved's name—be sure to include their last name too. What new revelations do you find?

November 27

Show appreciation for the love you would have never known without your beloved. Their presence is still felt in the unbreakable bond you share. Each pang of longing is a testament to the profound love and joy they brought into your life. Feel grateful for the love that never leaves and the connection that endures.

❤ **INVITATION:** Take breaks throughout your day to intentionally connect with your beloved, perhaps telling them: *Because I was loved by you* ... and see that words come next.

November 28

Water, whether in the form of tears, rain, or bodies like rivers and oceans, can have significant healing properties. Its flow mirrors the emotional currents of grief, reminding you that feelings come and go, and that renewal is a dynamic process.

❤ **INVITATION:** Visit a body of water—a river, lake, or even a fountain. Spend time there observing its movements and journaling about your beloved. Write about the parallels you see between the water and your own emotional topography.

November 29

Catastrophizing during grief is common because our minds try to prepare for the worst, hoping to shield us from pain. Grief leaves us vulnerable and our brain instinctively anticipates danger. However, this mindset deepens helplessness and anxiety, trapping us in a cycle of fear. If you're catastrophizing, answer yourself in writing: What is the worst outcome? The best? The most likely? What are the options in between? Examining this on paper can help shift your mindset from apprehension and inability to logic and empowerment.

♥ **INVITATION:** Write down a comforting thought and place it somewhere visible, and when your mind spirals, repeat it until calmness returns.

November 30

Is there a part of your grief you're avoiding? Something tucked away in the shadows, hoping it will fade? It's natural to distance yourself from grief to focus on work, family, or survival. Yet, it's equally important to confront it. Facing what you've avoided is frightening and requires immense strength. Even if you can't see it, your grief is teaching you about the courage and resilience within you.

♥ **INVITATION:** Journal about one part of your grief you're avoiding. You don't have to fix, change, or take any action step related to it; your acknowledgment is enough.

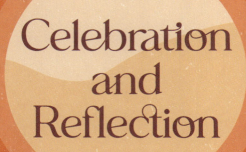

If you've been enduring an extended period of emotional nightfall, healing may feel slow. It may feel as if the pain of losing your beloved will never go away. While it is a pain that never truly disappears, it is something that you will eventually learn to move with in love. Seek guidance and wisdom during this sacred time to help you deepen your connection with your beloved. Also, allow yourself to reflect and reassure yourself that there is no time limit on your grief. You may feel an influx of emotions, flutters of happiness, sadness, fury, and sometimes a combination of emotions.

You may feel inspired to set intentions for the New Year, meet expectations during festive celebrations, or seek quiet reflection. If stress from self-criticism, budgeting, or holiday traditions arises, remember to take moments for self-recharge. It's okay if you can't be as present as before; lean on self-compassion and the comforting presence of your beloved to restore you.

If you are struggling, it is important to seek help from professionals and/or family and friends.

It's also okay to feel happiness and joy during these times. Embrace the pivot point between darkness and light this time of year, acknowledging the dualities in your grief and allowing yourself to nurture them.

December 1

If you'll be gathering with others this upcoming holiday season, consider weaving ways into your celebration to honor their beloveds as well. Offering a space for others to celebrate their companions can be a loving legacy for you and yours.

♥ **INVITATION:** Make an honoring tree where people can write their beloved's names on decorations, hang a gratitude bulletin board where people can express "thank-yous" to their companions, or stock a cookie decorating station with animal shapes to make tribute portrait cookies as a take-home favor.

December 2

It's an act of kindness to release the pressure of grieving "correctly." You're new to this—it's scary and inundating. You didn't choose this path, but here you are. Some days might show "progress," while others feel stuck. Remember, all stagnation ends, little by little. Grieving is tender, not wasted time. Relinquish the idea of doing it a certain way and commit to doing it your way. Only compare who you are now to who you used to be. Don't outshine other grievers—outshine yourself.

♥ **INVITATION:** Write yourself a permission slip that begins with *I allow myself to not do this aspect of my grief "correctly . . ."*

December 3

Many parts of your life won't return to how they "were." A gift of kindness to yourself is accepting this truth. Some activities, relationships, and behaviors might not serve you anymore. Clinging to who you were could mean missing new people, passions, and interests that elevate your life now. Release the pressure to restore to the past, and embrace new possibilities.

♥ **INVITATION:** Dive into a new skill, hobby, or community. These might become surprising lifelines.

December 4

Music can be a powerful link between you and your beloved. Does your beloved have a theme song? If not, now's the time to select one! You may even enjoy curating an entire playlist of songs that remind you of your beloved. You might also include songs with your beloved's names in them you've never heard of before. Activate this playlist when you're driving, cleaning, or walking in your favorite places to boost your connection with your beloved.

♥ **INVITATION:** Find an upbeat song that brings you joy and have a dance party with your beloved.

December 5

Holidays often reawaken the pain of loss. Embracing celebrations with self-care and remembrance can bring solace. Allow yourself to feel all emotions without the apprehension that you're "ruining" a holiday or betraying your beloved. Grieving during the holidays doesn't mean you're not appreciative of present moments with family and friends. It's okay to step back from festivities if you need space to honor your needs.

♥ **INVITATION:** Make a list of three ways you might like things to go differently during your holiday celebrations that would feel more authentic for your grief.

December 6

It's tempting to imagine that our beloved is the best relationship that we will ever have and that no other animal will ever compare. However, it might feel more supportive to dismantle the idea of a hierarchy with our beloveds and instead imagine a snowball. Each companion becomes part of the larger story of your evolution and growth as a guardian. Each of their gifts, guidance, lessons, and teachings are unique and add to a colossal, radiant, and ever-growing snowball of love, loyalty, and support.

♥ **INVITATION**: What are the many amazing insights wrapped up inside your snowball of animals you've loved?

December 7

Every time you think of something you'd like to share with your beloved, feel free to write it down or speak it aloud to them! One way to expand on this is to print favorite photos of your beloved. Every day, write a love note on the back of each that shares something about your life together: a gratitude, a memory, or anything you want your beloved to hear.

♥ **INVITATION**: Incorporate these love notes as part of your upcoming holiday traditions, like tucking them in your beloved's Christmas stocking, reading one on each night of Hanukkah, or using them as a special garland at a gathering.

December 8

Sharing the details of the uniqueness of your relationship, your beloved's quirky habit, a hilarious shenanigan, a must-do routine, or a memorable adventure can help you feel uplifted in your feelings and honor your beloved's legacy. Each time you speak your beloved's name and story into the world, you're gifting the universe with their powerful imprint.

♥ **INVITATION:** Say this to yourself quietly or aloud: *I embrace opportunities to celebrate my beloved's spirit.*

December 9

If you notice yourself speaking unkindly to yourself in your grief, ask yourself: *Would my beloved ever speak to me like this?* The first step to supporting this is to start listening to the way we talk about ourselves. Each time you catch your inner critic bullying you, begin speaking out loud to yourself the way you would to someone you truly love. Even if you don't "believe" it, fake it till you make it.

♥ **INVITATION:** Write a letter from your beloved to you, reminding you of all the things they love about you.

December 10

Why honor your beloved with their own holiday tree? It keeps them front and center! You can choose a tree or lights with your animal's signature color and enjoy curating ornaments that reflect different aspects of their life and personality. You can include their favorite treats, toys, sacred items, or ornaments from signs they've been sending. If you're not up for it, that's okay too. Respect where you are.

♥ **INVITATION:** If you were going to choose one signature ornament for your beloved, what would it be?

December 11

Grief is lonely. You're the only person in the world who knows what your beloved means to your daily routine and heart. Remember that you're sharing your grief right now with millions of others who are also mourning their beloveds. You're in a community of people who are waking up with similar challenges. The empathy and compassion you feel for others who are grieving can help support your own feelings of patience, understanding, and thoughtfulness for yourself. You are not alone.

♥ **INVITATION:** Say this to yourself quietly or aloud: *I honor my pain and the pain of all grieving guardians everywhere.*

December 12

Milestone days can feel like crossing a bridge into new emotional terrain. Consider the meaning of this crossing and how you wish to maneuver it. Milestones are yours to define, whether through reflection, honoring your beloved with self-care, or sharing their memory. Welcome family, friends, or community to join in marking the day, perhaps through gathering, sharing stories, or cooking your beloved's favorite food. Letting others know in advance encourages supportive gestures and reminds you that you're not alone.

♥ **INVITATION:** Consider notifying your circle. *My beloved's milestone is on [date]. Please check in with me that day so I can feel your support.*

December 13

If your beloved adored holiday season cuisine, keep them included with photo-infused delicacies! Cake pops, cookies, and even crème brûlée can all highlight images of your beloved. And, custom wine or sparkling cider can also feature your favorite image of your beloved, perfect for your next gathering's toast.

♥ **INVITATION:** Admire your beloved at an upcoming gathering through a photo-infused treat.

December 14

The holiday season is often synonymous with joy and even still, it's important to recognize your challenges. Your grief can create a deep sense of emptiness, especially during festive times. Treat yourself tenderly. If social events feel tough, it's okay to take a step back and seek comfort in quieter environments. Surround yourself with those who understand and respect your need for space and healing.

♥ **INVITATION:** Alert those in your community that you may need to experience upcoming events differently, so expectations are clear when you arrive or when you need to skip.

December 15

Talking to oneself in the mirror is a proven tool for self-compassion and emotional support, especially during grief. Research shows that mirror affirmations regulate emotions and reinforce positive thinking, activating brain areas linked to self-awareness and empathy. The "power pose"—standing confidently with hands on hips—also reduces stress hormones and boosts empowerment when combined with affirmations.

♥ **INVITATION:** As a daily practice, stand before a mirror, taking a confident stance. Make eye contact and say phrases like, *I honor my grief and my strength*, or *I am worthy of care and compassion*.

December 16

Using the grief feelings wheel on page 221, connect with the core emotions at the center. Are some emotions easy to access, while others feel distant or blocked? Notice what stirs these feelings within you and how they show up in your body. Have you been taught to shy away from certain emotions or feel shame around them? Gently explore where these beliefs come from and how they affect your ability to connect with your emotions during this time of grief.

♥ **INVITATION:** Journal about how each core emotion feels in your body and when you notice it the most.

December 17

With the focus on your beloved during their final day, it's difficult to meet your own needs. You may have struggled to be present, calm, clear-headed, or you may not have been able to attend. Whatever your own experience was on that last day, you deserve to have it supported and nurtured.

♥ **INVITATION:** Write a letter of self-compassion to yourself about how hard that last day was. Speak to yourself with the voice of a wise, loving friend. Offer yourself tenderness, affirmation, and love.

December 18

Sit quietly and breathe deeply. Think about how many numbers there are in your beloved's name, a special date, or the number of days you spent together earthside. Imagine these numbers holding a unique energy, glowing softly. Sense their presence—do they feel like strength, love, or peace? Let their energy flow through you.

♥ **INVITATION:** Research the numerology behind these numbers and reflect on their meanings. Incorporate them into small rituals—create a piece of art using these numbers, trace them in sand or soil, or collect that many nature items (leaves, stones) as an offering to honor your connection.

December 19

You may detect parts of yourself that have been hidden beneath layers of expectation and routine. These veiled aspects of your identity are integral to who you are. Surveying them with wonder, rather than judgment, can lead to a deeper connection with your true self. You are a complex and multifaceted being, worthy of understanding and love.

♥ **INVITATION:** Journal about parts of yourself that you rarely inspect. What passions, memories, or dreams have been set aside? How do these aspects of self influence who you are today and how might you cultivate them moving forward?

December 20

Just as a dolphin rises for air, you can also create moments of relief during grief. Close your eyes and embody the dolphin. Inhale deeply and exhale forcefully, imagining yourself breaking the surface, releasing heaviness with each breath. Do this ten times, feeling lighter with every exhalation. While you can't control your loss, you can choose thoughts that guide you through the darkness, empowering your spirit to breathe and heal gently.

❤ **INVITATION:** What is a helpful six-word thought you can write down today to return to when you need a lift?

December 21

If part of celebrations with your beloved included purchasing gifts for them, feel free to continue that tradition. Don't deny yourself the festive connection of gift giving if it feels supportive—choosing presents is a loving act of care and nurturing.

❤ **INVITATION:** Select and wrap a present for your beloved. When it's time for the celebration, you can decide who opens it, if you'd like to keep it on your beloved's altar, or if you'd prefer to donate it to a shelter or rescue after opening.

December 22

Some grief moments are heavier than others. If today feels like too much, gently place both hands over your heart and close your eyes. Feel the warmth of your beloved's love, always alive within you. Say their name out loud, three times, slowly. Let their name fill the space, reminding you of the power, connection, and infinity of your bond. Draw strength from their courage, their love, and their presence, knowing they are still with you, always guiding and reassuring you.

♥ **INVITATION:** Take a moment to hold something that reminds you of your beloved—a favorite toy, blanket, or photo. Let it ground you in their love and connection.

December 23

In the wake of your beloved's transition, it's natural to search for someone or something to blame. But blame can feel like carrying a heavy stone that weighs down your heart. Buddhist teachings remind us of impermanence—everything, including our beloveds, is subject to change. This perspective empowers us to move beyond fault, seeing transitioning as a natural part of life. By embracing compassion and mindfulness, you can gently set down the burden of blame and honor the enduring love you share.

♥ **INVITATION:** Write what you're blaming yourself for on a small piece of paper, then safely burn, bury, or destroy it as a symbol of relieving that suffering.

December 24

Close your eyes and take a deep breath. As you exhale, silently say to yourself: *Today, I will honor my beloved.* Breathe one more time, and at the exhalation say: *Today, I will embrace peace and love.* On your last breath say: *Today, I will be kind to myself.* Let each phrase envelop you with calm and love as you carry your beloved's spirit with you today.

♥ **INVITATION:** Write down your favorite *Today, I will . . .* statements and either repeat them throughout the day or keep them in a note in your phone as friendly reminders.

December 25

Allow this holiday season to feel different, and release expectations about how it "should" feel. Of course, you aren't going to feel "better" or "get over it" just because it's a holiday. But, acknowledging, feeling, and advocating for your grief, no matter how hard, is key. If you don't, it will wait inside and then pounce on you when you least expect it. Limit your obligations and make plenty of time to rest and nurture your grief.

♥ **INVITATION:** What special ritual can you create that honors your beloved today?

December 26

The idea of hope can sometimes be repulsive during grief. When it feels possible, welcome a gentle anticipation of good that is yet to come. Even on the most intense days, trust your inner wisdom to believe a time may come when light will break through.

♥ **INVITATION:** Carry hope in a tangible form. Choose an object—a crystal, an heirloom, or a photo—that embodies possible future goodness for you. Let it serve as an unceasing reminder of your developing relationship with hope.

December 27

You may find yourself dwelling on comments, memories, doubts, or heartaches that feel hard to shed. Sometimes, unburdening yourself from these thoughts can be freeing. Painful questions or events may have no answers, but releasing them can bring relief. When an upsetting thought or question arises, try writing it down on a small piece of paper.

♥ **INVITATION:** Create a "Universe Box" (or God Box, Surrender Box, or Turn It Over Box). Physically place each concern into this vessel and trust that it's being addressed. When it's full, release all the papers in a ritual of your choice.

December 28

Acknowledge the self-care practices or growth areas that have emerged since your beloved's transition. How has your beloved contributed—through companionship, lessons, or love to each one of these practices or growth areas? Take a moment to appreciate your beloved's continued influence in your life and remind yourself that you are deserving of all the good things that come into your life.

💜 **INVITATION:** List out all the self-care practices or growth areas that have emerged since your beloved's transition, noting how your beloved contributed to each. Keep this list nearby as a reminder of how their presence still nurtures and inspires you.

December 29

As everyone gears up for year-in-reviews and resolutions, you might feel out of sync, and that's okay. Flipping the calendar doesn't flip our feelings. New Year's Day can make our beloved's absence feel sharper, but grief isn't tied to time. It lingers, reminding us of the love we share and the possibility of ongoing connection in the New Year.

💜 **INVITATION:** What signs would you love to receive from your beloved in the upcoming New Year? Pen a request letter with the synchronicities you'll be looking for, such as repeating numbers, songs, colors, creatures, or words.

December 30

Remember that time is a human invention and your relationship with your beloved is everlasting. Nothing has to change about how you connect with, honor, or live your beloved's legacy just because a calendar year has advanced.

♥ **INVITATION:** Make a list of twenty collaborations with your beloved you would like to complete in the New Year. You two might learn a new skill together, travel to a new place together, help an animal in need, or complete a big project. What's on the horizon for the two of you?

December 31

Repeat this affirmation to yourself this New Year's Eve: *I deserve to grieve fully and openly. I release grief ideas that do not serve me. I am excited to continue my connection with my beloved and I am proud of our relationship. I will collaborate with my beloved and remain open to the possibilities this New Year brings.*

♥ **INVITATION:** Set an intention to release one major feeling or challenge grief has brought you this year and liberate it at midnight through shouting it, writing it and burying it, or imagining it floating into the sky.

Grieving Guardian Glossary

BELOVED: This is the term I use for all animal companions. Some people love "fur baby," "child," "pet," "partner," or "soulmate." I like the term "beloved" because it reflects how dear they are to us as an included member of our family.

CONNECT TO/WITH YOUR BELOVED: I use "connect to your beloved" often throughout instead of your beloved being "gone" or "lost." Instead of believing your relationship has ended, I advocate for connecting and tuning in with your beloved. This can be as simple as speaking out loud to them, writing to them, or going on a walk with their presence in mind. I believe each of us has the power to connect with our beloved through our deep wisdom and understanding of them and our connection—you are the only one who can truly know, hear, and connect with them.

EARTHSIDE PRESENCE: Because I believe our relationship continues to evolve and expand beyond the physical duration of our beloved's earthly body, I refer to their physical presence as "earthside" time as opposed to implying they are not "here." I believe our beloveds live in us, we live their legacy, and we can continue to nurture our bond with them beyond their earthside time.

GUARDIAN: The most common word, "owner," implies our beloveds are property. While that may be a legal definition, I like the term "guardian" because our role embodies so much more than ownership.

MOVE WITH: I say "move with" our grief as opposed to the idea of "moving on" or even "moving through." While we certainly are never "finished" grieving, we can feel relief from some of the acute, early grief symptoms and emotions we feel. There is not a "destination" to move to, move from, or move through to. Grief is a part of us forever and we work to adjust to and integrate it into our lives as we and our relationships with our beloveds continue to evolve.

ONGOING RELATIONSHIP: We don't leave our beloveds behind or detach from their gifts, lessons, and love. We keep them with us as we mature and our relationship evolves with us.

TRANSITION: The words "death" or "died" can feel harsh to some grievers, and euphemisms like "passed away," "went to sleep," "left," or "said goodbye" can feel inaccurate. I like "transition" because it reminds me that our beloved's physical presence has changed, and what we make of our future chapter with them is up to us.

WE: This is a collaboration mindset for you and your beloved! "We" are going for a walk; "we" are conquering our fear of heights. Staying in a "we" mindset with your beloved means the two of you can continue to journey through life together as a pair.

Grief Feelings Wheel

Index

Use this index as a tool to guide you toward meditations and invitations that resonate with your feelings or support your unique grief experience.

A

Absence, 17, 62
Adopting Again, 31, 55, 81, 123, 161, 194
Affirmations, 15, 18, 30, 34, 42, 47, 67, 72, 78, 86, 88, 108, 112, 117, 119, 135, 139, 193, 207, 208, 210, 215, 218
Afterlife, 20, 28, 109, 182
Ambiguous Loss, 35
Anger, 36, 55, 87, 106, 132, 185
Anticipatory Grief, 137
Anxiety, 146, 176, 180, 198
Art, 22, 24, 80, 86, 87, 93, 141, 142, 152, 157, 162, 173, 178
Asking for Help, 33, 59, 73, 112
Authenticity, 41, 51, 55, 59, 92, 103, 109, 144, 171, 175, 192, 205
Avoiding, 198

B

Bandwidth, 21, 89, 105, 194
Beliefs, 51, 124, 138, 143, 163, 179, 182, 190
Beloved's Belongings, 23, 29, 48, 68, 76, 87, 133, 161
Beloved's Remains, 125
Betrayal, 31, 119, 137, 185
Blame, 22, 67, 85, 118, 214
Body, 22, 52, 64, 80, 107, 110, 144, 146, 165, 176, 185

Both/And Thinking, 172
Boundaries, 21, 39, 89, 92, 95, 103, 110, 121, 154, 171, 177
Brain, 15, 19, 21, 50, 80, 90, 110, 146, 173, 198, 210,
Breathing, 20, 30, 39, 49, 100, 124, 133, 138, 141, 176, 195, 213

C

Catastrophizing, 198
Challenges, 77, 107, 156, 210
Change, 69, 187
Children, 54, 58, 166
Collaborating, 49, 61, 103, 146, 168, 218
Comfort, 11, 12, 15, 20, 37, 38, 39, 60, 66, 72, 76, 80, 82, 104, 109, 112, 153, 162, 169
Community, 23, 33, 59, 69, 73, 77, 105, 112, 208
Comparison, 40, 52, 93, 128, 171, 206
Connecting, 12, 20, 31, 34, 36, 37, 39, 48, 51, 53, 57, 59, 60, 62, 65, 68, 74, 78, 80, 83, 101, 103, 104, 109, 110, 112, 129, 131, 133, 138, 143, 151, 158, 173, 176, 184, 193, 195, 197, 212, 214, 215
Control, 29, 69, 85, 136
Coping, 50, 116

Creativity, 14, 17, 22, 24, 29, 31, 32, 48, 58, 62, 65, 66, 68, 81, 82, 86, 99, 101, 110, 112, 116, 128, 129, 134, 146, 153, 157, 159, 161, 164, 169, 173, 182, 203, 205, 208, 209
Crying, 88, 176
Cultivating Joy, 21, 81, 104, 113, 116, 117, 164

D
Decision Making, 23, 144
Decluttering, 108
Distraction, 116, 160
Dreams, 19, 165

E
Emotions, 24, 25, 26, 54, 94, 100, 109, 111, 119, 123, 137, 140, 155, 172, 174, 176, 182, 211
Empowerment, 29, 36, 39, 50, 62, 69, 107, 144
Euthanasia, 122
Expectations, 38

F
Fear, 178, 189, 198
Fear of Forgetting, 24, 137, 184
First Of The Month, 168
Firsts, 47
Flexibility, 134, 195
Future, 23, 38, 42, 60, 99, 127, 156, 164, 168, 177, 179, 189, 191, 204, 212, 216

G
Gotcha Day, 24, 64, 147, 194
Gratitude, 34, 50, 69, 71, 85, 136, 141, 192, 196, 197
Grief Expressions, 38, 81, 88, 101, 102
Grief Feelings Wheel, 25, 100, 123, 140, 155, 165, 182, 211
Grief Wins, 91
Grieving, 71, 94, 102, 124, 130, 152, 160, 162, 187
Grounding, 144
Guilt, 31, 56, 67, 85, 114, 132, 157, 163, 170, 191

H
Hard Days, 20, 56, 61, 114, 138, 139, 153, 193, 213, 214
Helping Others, 33, 49, 64, 69, 91, 93, 111, 119
Hobbies, 19, 104, 204
Holidays, 34, 42, 85, 117, 181, 183, 188, 203, 205, 206, 208, 209, 210, 213, 215, 217, 218
Honoring, 11, 12, 14, 17, 29, 31, 32, 37, 38, 48, 65, 66, 68, 71, 80, 81, 82, 83, 86, 87, 91, 92, 101, 104, 122, 125, 126, 128, 130, 134, 137, 153, 154, 158, 159, 161, 164, 170, 175, 187, 189, 196, 203, 208, 212, 215
Hope, 60, 189, 216

I
Identity, 13, 38, 51, 57, 90, 121, 130, 135, 142, 145, 177, 204, 212
Inner Child, 159
Inner Voice, 139
Integrating, 142
Intention, 13, 36, 37, 48, 53, 57, 60, 62, 70, 74, 83, 94, 111, 126, 142, 158, 160, 181, 189, 197, 218

L
Last Earthside Day, 11, 56, 122, 157, 169, 211
Laughter, 21, 81, 186
Legacy, 33, 34, 48, 91, 126
Life Lessons, 41, 48, 71, 72, 92, 107, 119, 131, 155
Loneliness, 59, 78, 158, 208

M
Meaning, 72, 163
Memories, 20, 24, 37, 57, 59, 70, 77, 80, 182, 186, 193, 194
Milestones, 64, 134, 147, 209
Mindfulness, 18, 22, 47, 61, 83, 88, 100, 110, 111, 129, 141, 153, 163, 165, 174, 176, 214
Missing Companion, 35
Movement, 132, 146, 185
Moving, 87
Moving On, 32, 93
Multiple Losses, 186
Music, 62, 82, 146, 205

N
Nature, 36, 54, 57, 61, 70, 93, 133, 197
Nighttime, 37, 120, 190

O
Overreacting, 58
Overwhelm, 18, 25, 26, 61, 105, 114, 155, 213

P
Pain, 65
People Pleasing, 92, 109, 171
Perfectionism, 84
Permission Slip, 21, 28, 40, 52, 74, 81, 88, 89, 125, 143, 172, 175, 183, 204
Phone, 28, 37, 51, 159
Place, 22, 29, 30, 48, 76, 82, 87, 108, 113, 139, 169
Play, 36, 122, 186, 196
Privacy, 121
Projection, 181
Purpose, 13, 193

Q
Questioning, 16, 20, 23, 30, 35, 70, 72, 132, 145, 152, 154, 182, 190, 216

R
Regret, 67, 70, 132, 170, 174, 176
Relationships, 23, 33, 41, 55, 59, 69, 73, 75, 81, 84, 92, 95, 102, 103, 112, 118, 152, 154, 158, 160, 171, 172, 177, 179, 183, 196, 206, 209
Release, 18, 31, 35, 36, 38, 54, 65, 77, 94, 109, 114, 118, 132, 189, 218

Reparenting, 192
Resilience, 13, 82, 86, 107, 126, 190
Responding vs Reacting, 29, 111
Reunion, 109
Right Here, Right Now, 13, 18, 41, 100, 174
Rituals, 37, 74, 82, 83, 87, 94, 120, 129, 143, 153, 159, 175, 190, 195, 216
Roles, 75, 103, 178
Routines, 12, 120, 180

S
Secondary Losses, 14
Self-Care, 52, 60, 62, 64, 66, 67, 75, 83, 89, 93, 100, 108, 110, 154, 217
Self-Compassion, 16, 55, 58, 70, 73, 75, 84, 90, 91, 108, 117, 124, 135, 138, 159, 170, 192, 193, 210, 211
Self-Criticism, 16, 22, 38, 40, 76, 84, 88, 117, 138, 159, 174, 191, 192, 204, 207
Self-Discovery, 19, 25, 26, 53, 57, 60, 66, 82, 104, 121, 128, 135, 139, 142, 144, 145, 162, 177, 179, 188, 191, 212, 217
Self-Forgiveness, 67
Self-Love, 39, 40, 41, 78, 108, 127, 129, 188
Sharing, 77, 207
Shoulding, 21, 40, 85, 215
Signs, 16, 19, 130, 171, 217
Soothing, 17, 18, 52, 109
Sound, 17, 28, 35, 173
Spirituality, 20, 28, 30, 53, 72, 106, 109, 113, 140, 145, 182, 189

Stuck, 56, 77, 155
Supportive Thoughts, 126
Survival, 13
Surviving Animals, 15, 106, 136, 180, 206

T
Traveling, 29, 76, 113

U
Unexpected Loss, 120, 156, 190
Universe, 28, 30, 106, 113, 216
Unsupportive Feedback, 40, 55, 84, 118, 121, 160, 172, 177
Unsupportive Thoughts, 22, 114, 216

V
Values, 13, 51

W
Word Choice, 40, 49, 102
Work, 89

Y
Your Beloved's Name, 14, 22, 35, 65, 122, 125, 170, 187, 196, 205, 212, 214

Acknowledgments

To all the beloved companions who have enriched the lives of my clients, community, and readers of this book: Thank you. Thank you for nurturing, transforming, and grounding us. Thank you for being our anchor, protector, and adventure partner. Thank you for your roles as reparent, cheerleader, healer, teacher, and lifeboat, showing us the strength of unwavering connection and adoration. We are so lucky to be your family.

To every grieving guardian I've had the privilege to encounter, your resilience through heartbreak, courage amid loss, and enduring love inspire my work and deepen my commitment to honoring these sacred bonds. Thank you for sharing your beloveds, stories, and truths with me.

To my heart cat, Zelda: Thank you for teaching me boundaries, patience, loyalty, the promise of possibility, and the beauty of pájaros. Your wisdom resonates within me daily.

And to my soulmate, Arnie: Thank you for the gift of your life, which has made my own possible. You were my light and strength when I needed it most and our soul connection is a wellspring, nourishing my spirit and work each day. Thank you for collaborating with me on our mission to support, normalize, and validate pet loss grief. I can't wait to see where we go next.

About the Author

Beth Bigler is a double-certified Pet Loss Grief Counselor, end-of-life animal companion doula, and pet chaplain dedicated to helping guardians honor the profound bonds they share with their beloved animals. After experiencing the sudden death of her soulmate cat, Arnie, Beth transformed her grief into a compassionate mission: guiding others to validate their experience, connect with their beloveds, and integrate grief into their lives. As the founder of Honoring Our Animals, Beth is one of the world's leading voices in pet loss support, offering personalized care to individuals and families before, during, and after their beloved's transition. An entertainment industry veteran, Beth enjoyed a twenty-year career as a writer, producer, and educator for stage, page, film, and television. Connect with Beth at www.honoringouranimals.com or on Instagram @honoringouranimals.

© 2025 by Quarto Publishing Group USA Inc.
Text © 2025 by Beth Bigler

First published in 2025 by Wellfleet Press, an imprint of The Quarto Group, 142 West 36th Street, 4th Floor, New York, NY 10018, USA
(212) 779-4972 www.Quarto.com

All rights reserved. No part of this book may be reproduced in any form without written permission of the copyright owners. All images included in this book are original works created by the artist credited on the copyright page, not generated by artificial intelligence, and have been reproduced with the knowledge and prior consent of the artist. The producer, publisher, and printer accept no responsibility for any infringement of copyright or otherwise arising from the contents of this publication. Every effort has been made to ensure that credits accurately comply with information supplied. We apologize for any inaccuracies that may have occurred and will resolve inaccurate or missing information in a subsequent reprinting of the book.

Wellfleet titles are also available at discount for retail, wholesale, promotional, and bulk purchase. For details, contact the Special Sales Manager by email at specialsales@quarto.com or by mail at The Quarto Group, Attn: Special Sales Manager, 100 Cummings Center Suite 265D, Beverly, MA 01915 USA.

10 9 8 7 6 5 4 3 2 1

ISBN: 978-1-57715-514-0

Digital edition published in 2025
eISBN: 978-0-7603-9536-3

Library of Congress Control Number: 2024951272

Group Publisher: Rage Kindelsperger
Editorial Director: Erin Canning
Creative Director: Laura Drew
Managing Editor: Cara Donaldson
Editor: Keyla Pizarro-Hernández
Cover and Interior Design: Raine Rath

Printed in China

This book provides general information on various widely known and widely accepted images and content that tend to evoke feelings of strength and confidence. However, it should not be relied upon as recommending or promoting any specific diagnosis or method of treatment for a particular condition, and it is not intended as a substitute for medical or mental health advice or for direct diagnosis and treatment of a medical or mental health condition by a qualified physician. Readers who have questions about a particular condition, possible treatments for that condition, or possible reactions from the condition or its treatment should consult a physician or other qualified health care professional.

Use great caution when working with fire by having plenty of water or a fire extinguisher at the ready.